The Inevitable Party

The Inevitable Party

Why Attempts to Kill the Party System Fail and How they Weaken Democracy

SETH E. MASKET

OXFORD
UNIVERSITY PRESS

OXFORD
UNIVERSITY PRESS

Oxford University Press is a department of the University of Oxford. It furthers
the University's objective of excellence in research, scholarship, and education
by publishing worldwide. Oxford is a registered trade mark of Oxford University
Press in the UK and certain other countries.

Published in the United States of America by Oxford University Press
198 Madison Avenue, New York, NY 10016, United States of America.

Library of congress cataloging in publication data
Names: Masket, Seth E., 1969– author.
Title: The inevitable party : why attempts to kill the party system fail and how they weaken
democracy/ Seth E. Masket.
Description: New York, NY : Oxford University Press, 2016. | Includes bibliographical references.
Identifiers: LCCN 2015041699 (print) | LCCN 2016001172 (ebook) | ISBN 978-0-19-022083-9
(hardcover : alk. paper) | ISBN 978-0-19-022084-6 (pbk. : alk. paper) | ISBN 978-0-19-022085-3
(E-book) | ISBN 978-0-19-060844-6 (Online Component) Subjects: LCSH: Political parties—
United States—History—20th century. | Progressivism (United States politics)—History—20th
century. | Political culture—United States—History—20th century. | U.S. states—Politics and
government. Classification: LCC JK2261 .M355 2016 (print) | LCC JK2261 (ebook) | DDC 324.273—
dc23 LC record available at http://lccn.loc.gov/2015041699

9 8 7 6 5 4 3 2
Printed by Sheridan, USA

CONTENTS

ACKNOWLEDGMENTS

At an early stage of the research that would become this book, I was on the phone with Rob Witwer, a former Colorado statehouse representative and an author of a book about campaign finance. I was trying to trace some financial transactions from 527s, and I knew Witwer had done some of this for his book, so I was hoping he could help me. We ended up talking on the phone for about an hour while he led me on a frustrating and ultimately unsuccessful hunt through state financial disclosures, federal donation tracking pages, and the IRS's website. Ultimately, Witwer stopped and said, "You're a political scientist. I used to be in the statehouse. If we can't figure this out, who is this for?"

This question has remained at the forefront of my mind throughout this project. In an earlier book, *No Middle Ground*, I focused on the causes of partisan polarization. This subject still interests me greatly, but I have been impressed with the amount of attention and effort being devoted to attempting to reverse polarization. It's notable that people have come to perceive polarization as a problem in need of immediate solution, but many of the proposed solutions have struck me as short-sighted, uninformed by history, and unconcerned with the positive aspects of political parties or in the general principal of unintended consequences.

This book has benefited massively from many broad, conceptual discussions about parties and reforms, principally with Hans Noel, Jennifer Nicoll Victor, Julia Azari, and Gregory Koger. John Zaller has continued to encourage and inspire me throughout this project, and his enthusiasm for my Nebraska research was particularly helpful at an early stage. I like to think I know what I'm doing in social network research, but then I start using R and everything goes to hell. And that's where I got vital guidance from Skyler Cranmer and Philip Leifeld.

The various case studies in this book began with me essentially as a tourist, trying to learn a great deal about state political systems over a very short period of time. I am deeply grateful to those who offered their time and advice, and especially to those who opened their homes to me during my visits.

My work on the Colorado chapter rests heavily on some pioneering work done by Rob Witwer and Adam Schrager. I received valuable feedback on early drafts of this work from Thad Kousser and Daniel Smith.

For the Nebraska chapter, I relied heavily on Boris Shor's data collections and many discussions we had over their implications. Amanda Friesen, Michael Wagner, and Ari and Sara Kohen were gracious and helpful hosts during my field research there. I've benefited from a great deal of feedback on this chapter from Kevin Collins, James Fowler, Daniel Galvin, Georgia Kernell, Nolan McCarty, Betsy Sinclair, and Craig Volden. Field research for this chapter was supported by a Faculty Research Fund award from the University of Denver.

For the Minnesota research, I received some very thoughtful assistance from John Aldrich and Marjorie Hershey. Philip Chen, Kate McClenny, Emily Richard, Lindsay Roberts, and Emmanuel Rubio provided help with data entry. I am particularly grateful to Robbie LaFleur and the staff of the Minnesota Legislative Reference Library for helping me find interest group ratings.

The research on California's recall election spanned many years, and was aided immeasurably by lengthy conversations with and gracious invitations from Lark Park and Jimmy Evans. I received a great deal of useful guidance from Sheri Annis, Clea Benson, Joe Doherty, Wesley Hussey, Marc Herman, Justin Phillips, and Richard Skinner.

In Wisconsin, I received thoughtful feedback from Barry Burden, Eric McGhee, and Carol Weissert. Michael Davidson and Keith Poole provided vital help in extracting roll call votes from state legislative journals and converting them to ideal points. I received additional assistance and advice from Julia Azari, Martin Drafton, Keith Dougherty, Peter Hanson, Jenni Le, and Angelina Zaytsev. Samuel Kernell and Carl Klarner offered helpful data assistance.

I particularly appreciated some guidance and encouragement on my concluding chapter from Thomas Mann, Jim Thurber, and Antoine Yoshinaka. Karen Crummy was extremely helpful to me in interpreting campaign finance data.

More generally, I owe a debt of gratitude to the overlapping-but-not-exactly-concentric circles known as the Klugies, the UCLA School, and the Mischiefs of Faction. These include, but are not limited to, Julia Azari, Larry Bartels, Kathleen Bawn, Marty Cohen, Kristin Kanthak, David Karol, Gregory Koger, Jonathan Ladd, Scott McClurg, Joanne Miller, Hans Noel, John Patty, David Peterson, Darren Schreiber, Richard Skinner, Anand Sokhey, Jennifer Nicoll Victor, Christina Wolbrecht, and John Zaller. Through many, many discussions-some in conference rooms, some on-line, some over engraved flasks full of bourbon on the 23rd floor of the Palmer House Hilton-these folks helped me work through some of the findings of my research and their implications. My University of Denver colleagues Peter Hanson and Nancy Wadsworth were kind enough to read some early versions of this work and help me keep it on track. I am also deeply grateful to John Sides and the crew at the Monkey Cage at the *Washington Post*, Nicholas Jackson at *Pacific Standard*, and Ezra Klein and Matt Yglesias at *Vox. com* for giving me some space to write about and work through this research and receive valuable feedback. And I thank David McBride and the crew and anonymous reviewers at Oxford University Press for the detailed and thorough reads, the helpful feedback, and the great support for this project.

I must thank my parents Barbara and Sam Masket, my in-laws Paula and Stuart Boxer, my brother Harris Masket and his wife Sirena, and my sister-in-law Nora Boxer, who have asked me about this project enough to warrant free copies of the book. And of course, I leave my final thanks to my immediate family-Vivian, Eli, and Sadie-who continue to inspire me, encourage me, and make it all worth doing.

Fixing Politics

The actual consequences of party reform are, in the future as in the past, likely often to disappoint their advocates, relieve their opponents, and surprise a lot of commentators.

RANNEY (1975, 191)

Early 21st-century political journalists and reformers have spent no small amount of time complaining about the "jackass quotient" in American politics (Alter 2009). Our political system has simply become too polarized and too nasty, the arguments go. Politicians are increasingly ignoring the common good and instead focusing on their own narrow partisan interests or, worse, just acting spitefully to make the other side look bad. The result has been gridlock, a government that is either unwilling or unable to address the considerable challenges before it. And so the calls go out for something—anything—to reduce the polarization and somehow release our political system from the parties' death grip.

Plenty of solutions have been offered, including more parties, no parties, redistricting reform, bipartisan congressional retreats, and much more. One purported solution is a restructuring of primary elections. Primaries, after all, are the means by which most parties within the United States pick their nominees, and if the nominees are simply too extreme, maybe that's because of the donors, activists, and ideologically extreme voters who tend to dominate primary elections. In particular, if we could have open primaries, allowing independent and moderate voters to participate, perhaps the resulting party nominees would be more centrist and better able to compromise across party lines for the good of the nation.

One of the early testing grounds for this theory was the state of California. The Golden State's legislature has long been noted for being one of the most polarized in the nation (Shor and McCarty 2011) and, thanks in part to its unusual two-thirds budget vote requirement, one of the most paralyzed, as well (Masket 2009b). Reformers pinned part of the blame for this state of affairs on California's semiclosed primary system (Vocke 2010): primary elections were available only to registered party members, although unaffiliated voters could request one party's ballot on election day. Thus primary elections were dominated by the most partisan voters in the state, and politicians toed the party line to keep those primary voters happy.

In 2010, a coalition of reformers managed to collect enough signatures to place an initiative, known as Proposition 14, on the state ballot, creating a top-two primary for the state. Under the top-two system, any registered voter could participate in a primary, and all voters would see the same ballot, with all candidates of all parties appearing for each office. The top two vote-getters for each office would then go to a November runoff election, even if they were of the same party. In theory, this would encourage greater moderation among officeholders. If two Democrats appeared on a runoff ballot in San Francisco, the more moderate of the two would theoretically have better odds of winning, having an easier time winning over moderate and conservative voters in the district. As a *San Francisco Chronicle* op-ed claimed, the top-two reform would create "a system where representatives put what's best for California ahead of extreme partisan doctrine" (Buchanan and Jones 2010). A writer for the *Ventura County Star* similarly argued,

That's the quickest way to assure putting at least some moderate centrists into the state Legislature. It's also the quickest way to give a voice to millions of voters who now essentially have no representation in state government. And it's the first step toward making state government work better. (Elias 2009)

Backed by such high-profile figures as Governor Arnold Schwarzenegger and Lieutenant Governor Abel Maldonado (along with other moderate Republicans, who have had a difficult time obtaining and retaining office in California in recent years), Proposition 14 passed with the backing of 54 percent of voters in the June 2010 primary election. This reform went into effect in time for the 2012 primaries for state legislature and Congress. Early analyses, though, found little effect. The officeholders elected through this system didn't appear to be any more moderate than those elected under the previous system (Ahler, Citrin, and Lenz 2015; Kousser, Phillips, and Shor 2016; although see Grose 2014).

Why doesn't the reform seem to have worked? In part, because the state parties responded to it. Concerned that they were being dealt out of the game, both parties formalized a system of preprimary endorsements, picking their preferred candidates and broadcasting their choices on the state's primary election literature. These endorsements, it turns out, had a powerful effect on voters, boosting vote shares for endorsees by 10 to 15 percentage points (Kousser et al. 2015). What's more, candidates have come to appreciate the importance of these endorsements and now compete for them. The reform may have had the inadvertent effect of *increasing* the importance of parties in elections, especially if candidates compete for endorsements by taking more ideologically extreme stances to impress party leaders (Cahn 2013).

The above story is not a fluke. It has played out numerous times over many different party reform efforts—from direct primaries to campaign finance reform to nonpartisan elections—usually with the same disappointing outcome. The reason for this outcome, as I argue in this book, is that reform movements have consistently misunderstood and mischaracterized parties.

Parties are not rigid entities, limited to their appearances in legal definitions or business filings. They are, rather, networks of intense and creative policy demanders (Beck 1997; Cohen et al. 2008), working both inside and outside the government to determine the sort of people who get elected to office and thus change public policy. Making some aspect of party behavior illegal doesn't remove or necessarily even weaken parties; it just makes for a new business environment for the policy demanders. Limit their direct contributions to candidates, allow independents to participate in primaries, make a legislature nonpartisan, and so on, and they will still find a way to get the sorts of candidates they prefer nominated.

Parties are, quite simply, fiercely resilient entities, capable of adapting to reforms designed to weaken or kill them. But it is not so much that they are strong as that they are both endemic and essential to democratic governance. The argument laid out in this book is fundamentally consistent with Schattschneider's (1942) claim that modern democracy is unthinkable save in terms of parties. The history of party regulations in American politics is a testament to the fundamental truth of Schattschneider's claim. But parties are more than simply necessary, as I will argue; they are a positive force in a democracy. They establish grounds for debate, enable constructive criticism of a ruling regime, provide voters with policy alternatives, imbue elections with meaning, and allow for greater public involvement in the political system. I further argue that efforts to rein in or eliminate parties proceed from a misunderstanding of what parties are. Not only do they tend to misdiagnose the political system's problems and fail to constrain parties, but they tend to leave politics worse off for the effort.

This book certainly does not argue that regulation itself is a futile act. The state is quite clearly capable of limiting or banning undesirable activities. Tremendous energy is spent debating and protesting laws banning or permitting abortion, raising or lowering tax rates, deciding what must or must not be taught in public schools, and determining who may or may not marry, just to name a few areas, precisely because what is written in the legal codes matters. And the state has, on occasion, regulated party activities effectively (Harmel and Janda 1982), prohibiting racial discrimination in the selection of delegates or participation in primaries, for example.

But the state wades into a difficult area when it determines (as it does frequently) that parties are a fundamental problem for democracy and need to be curbed or eliminated. The Progressive Era was rife with attempts to rein in or eliminate parties. Between 1890 and 1920, federal and state governments passed laws regulating how party leaders and delegates were chosen and what sorts of conventions they must hold, established nonpartisan elections for most municipalities, and created direct primaries across the country (Ranney 1975). That same era saw the creation of a nonpartisan state legislature in Minnesota and cross-filing in California, which allowed candidates to run in multiple party primaries simultaneously. It also saw the birth of the direct open primary in Wisconsin and other states, seen as a way of disempowering party bosses by letting moderate voters, rather than party-loyal convention delegates, choose party nominees.

But that was hardly the end of such regulation. The late 1960s and early 1970s saw a spate of party reforms, largely aimed at making convention delegates and the nominees they chose more representative of the party rank-and-file and to wrest power from out-of-touch party bosses. Reforms in both parties led to an explosion in the number of state presidential primaries. Other reforms targeted campaign spending in an effort to reduce the influence of parties in elections by limiting their financial power. The Federal Election Campaign Act and later state and federal financial restrictions made it more difficult for parties to directly fund their nominees. The reformers that pressed those changes had an ally in the U.S. Supreme Court. Indeed, the same court that determined that campaign spending was a form of political free speech defended these abridgments of parties' speech rights out of a concern that party spending could "encourage candidate loyalty and responsiveness to the party"[1] (Rosenblum 2008). The past few years have seen another round of antiparty reforms, as well, including the top-two primaries adopted in Washington and California, as described above.

This is an impressive amount of legislative activity devoted to a fairly narrow range of perceived abuses. It also has an astonishingly bad track record. To be sure, laws affecting who may or may not participate in

1. *Federal Election Commission* v. *Democratic Senatorial Campaign Committee*, 454 U.S. 27 (1981).

party politics have been effective. The McGovern-Fraser reforms of the early 1970s, for example, dramatically changed the makeup of delegates at Democratic conventions. Gone were the uniform delegations of staid white male middle-aged party operatives. By 1972, many of them had been replaced by a delegation that looked "like a couple of high schools, a grape boycott, a Black Panther rally, and four or five politicians who walked in the wrong door," according to actress Shirley McClaine, herself a 1968 delegate from California (Ranney 1975). And at least for a while, the parties seemed to be nominating different sorts of candidates. George McGovern and Jimmy Carter did not seem to be the insiders' choices for the Democratic Party's presidential nomination in 1972 and 1976, respectively, but won it anyway.

Despite these differences in the most visible faces of the parties, the actual substance of party behavior in American politics, over the long run, changed very little in response to various reforms. Any ideological differences between candidates selected through open primaries and closed primaries are either meager (Gerber and Morton 1998; Kanthak and Morton 2001) or undetectable (McGhee et al. 2014). Figure 1.1 provides an example of this, charting the degree of legislative polarization in each state's lower house against the degree of openness in state legislative primaries. If more restrictive primary participation rules lead to more extreme state legislators, we would expect to see a downward slope to the trendline in the figure, with more open primaries being associated with less polarized legislatures. In fact, the trendline is nearly flat, with a slight *upward* tilt, suggesting that the more open primaries are somehow producing slightly more polarized legislators. The most straightforward interpretation, though, is that open primaries are simply failing to deliver on their promise of depolarizing politics.

Few other reforms have shown much success in affecting partisan politics, either. Decades of campaign finance reform have hardly diminished the role of money in politics, and the parties are now getting around campaign finance restrictions by creating or co-opting sympathetic 527 organizations or Super PACs that can provide unlimited funds to preferred candidates (Skinner, Masket, and Dulio 2012). Limiting party donations to candidates doesn't seem to be mitigating partisanship; it may actually

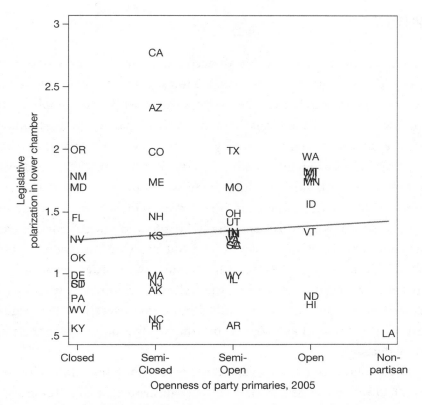

Figure 1.1 State Legislative Polarization as a Function of Party Primary Openness.
Note: The vertical axis charts the difference in party medians of ideal points for each state lower chamber in 2005 (Shor and McCarty 2013). The horizontal axis charts the degree of openness in state legislative party primaries as of 2005 (McGhee et al. 2014).

be increasing it (La Raja and Schaffner 2015). Today's nominees appear to be every bit the creatures of party insiders, with little evidence that reforms have disempowered party bosses (Cohen et al. 2008). And while the move to blanket primaries has occurred only recently in a few states, there is little reason to believe it will have a substantial impact on legislative polarization (McGhee 2010; McGhee et al. 2014).

This is not to say that antiparty reforms have no short-term effect. It may take parties some time to adapt to a new institutional regime. Sometimes they can adapt within one or two election cycles; other times it may take decades. But they almost always do adapt, emerging at least as strong as they were before the reform, and sometimes stronger. This result is highly instructive about the nature of parties.

WHY REFORM?

Given the rather paltry record of accomplishment of party reformers over the past century, it is reasonable to ask why they continue to try. Part of the answer is that they have an ever-willing accomplice: the American voter. Americans have never held parties in particularly high regard. Even many of a party's regular supporters refuse to identify themselves as members of that party (Keith et al. 1992). And even if most voters still affiliate with a party, we shouldn't confuse that with approval for parties in general. The survey evidence on this is mixed but leans negative: "Most have many hostile and few supportive feelings about the existing party system but most do not want it abolished" (Ranney 1975). The sentiments Ranney recorded seem to have grown more negative over time; the feeling thermometers used by the American National Election Studies show that overall public evaluation of the parties has dropped by roughly five points over the past three decades.

The second reason for the persistence of reform is that critics of parties have had very prominent leaders with persuasive arguments. These arguments have generally fallen into one of three main reformist critiques of parties, as summed up by Richard Hofstadter (1972, 12–13):

First, they often postulated that society should be pervaded by concord and governed by a consensus that approached, if it did not attain, unanimity. Party, and the malicious and mendacious spirit it encouraged, were believed only to create social conflicts that would not otherwise occur, or to aggravate dangerously those that normally would occur. . . . Second, a party or faction was very likely to become the instrument with which some small and narrow special interest could impose its will upon the whole of society, and hence to become the agent of tyranny. . . . Finally, the party, with its capacity to arouse malice and hostility and to command loyalty to a political entity much narrower and less legitimate than the "public good" as a whole, was considered to be a force directly counterposed to civic virtue.

The adherents of these tenets bear some of the most prominent names in American political history. George Washington warned against the "the baneful effects of the Spirit of Party" in his Farewell Address. James Madison worried, "No sooner has one party discovered or invented any amelioration of the condition of man, or the order of society than the opposite party belies it, misconstrues it, misrepresents it, ridicules it, insults it, and persecutes it" (quoted in Rosenblum 2008). Thomas Jefferson famously quipped, "If I could not go to heaven but with a party, I would not go there at all" (quoted in Rutland 1995). That Madison, Jefferson, and others would build parties of their own within a few years of uttering these sentences is immaterial for reformers.

The Founders hardly invented such antiparty sentiments—the Romans referred to parties as "the irrepressible hydra"—nor were they the sole purveyors of them in the United States. In response to the growth of urban party machines in the late 19th century, Populist and Progressive reformers argued about the evils of parties and promoted reforms, including home rule and the merit system, designed to break parties or make them obsolete. From the reformers' perspective, "the political parties stood directly in the path of the people's direct exercise of power and an efficiently run national community. They needed to be virtually eliminated" (DiSalvo 2012). Progressive journalist Lincoln Steffens proclaimed, "The party system is a device for the prevention of the expression of the common will; it misleads and obscures public opinion; it is simply another form of despotism" (1904, 11). Theodore Roosevelt (1906) gave fiery speeches depicting parties as criminal organizations that interceded between voters and their elected officials. Other reformers argued that the parties were only in power because of a reliance on poor, easily manipulated, immigrant voters; discouraging such votes would cause the machines to fall. Mosei Ostrogorski (Ostrogorski and Clarke 1902) famously described internal party governance as oligarchy.

Smith and Azari (2015) see these orators as part of a long antiparty movement that runs throughout (and even predates) American history. Whigs, Progressives, Perot supporters, Tea Partiers, and Americans Elect promoters are all examples of this political ideology, which vies with partyism for control of the American political system. The modern heirs of this antiparty ideology, from John McCain to Arnold Schwarzenegger to Arianna Huffington, continue to berate partisanship and to call for limitations on the role of parties in elections so that the voice of the people can be heard. Even the Supreme Court has determined that fealty to party is a democratic harm in need of regulation.[2] As Nancy Rosenblum notes, this pervasive antiparty ideology has led to the privileging of nonpartisans in American political culture. In just one example, a 2004 presidential debate featured a town-hall style format to which only undecided and independent voters were invited; loyal partisans were deemed to have insufficient standing to participate (Rosenblum 2008).

And who stands on the other side to defend modern parties as not only inevitable but actually good for democracy? Apart from a number of political scientists and Supreme Court Associate Justice Antonin Scalia, not many people. Schattschneider, one of the most vocal proponents of the importance of parties for democracy, once suggested that Americans could be educated to appreciate parties. "While the public has not yet been convinced" of parties' value, respond Harmel and Janda (1982, 98), "it would be difficult to argue that anyone has seriously tried to persuade them."

With such an impressive array of political and journalistic figures lined up in favor of some version of party reform, and so few lined up to defend the parties as they are, is it any wonder that reforms often pass, despite lack of evidence of their effectiveness? Every national malady becomes a complaint about the parties, and every failed reform is just evidence that more reform is needed.

THE COSTS OF REFORM

The reader may legitimately ask if such failed party reforms bear much of a societal cost. That is, apart from the wasted campaign resources (which, if they manage to engage some citizens in politics, aren't completely

---

2. *Federal Election Commission* v. *Colorado Republican Federal Campaign Committee*, 533 U.S. 431 (2001).

wasted), is there anything inherently wrong with at least sending a signal to policymakers about what an ideal form of government might look like? At least they're trying, we might note.

This is true, but it does ignore reform's more significant consequences. Just because antiparty reforms are not, in the long run, effective at reining in parties, that does not mean they have no impact on American democracy. What they tend to do is to make democracy less transparent.

Take campaign finance reform. It seems uncontroversial to say that efforts to limit spending in campaigns have hardly reduced the role of money in American politics. They *have* set hard legal limits on how much money parties and individuals may *directly* contribute to candidates. But placing a limit on how much a party or other donor can contribute to a candidate, in a familiar analogy, is like placing a hand in front of a stream of water; the water will find a way around. So long as there are donors seeking to contribute and candidates eager to spend, money will get from the former to the latter one way or another, and through innovations like political action committees, 527s, and independent expenditures, it does. As I demonstrate in chapter 3, a great deal of money gets from traditional Colorado Democratic Party donors to state legislative candidates via a web of 527s. This makes tracking individual donations far more difficult. With money flowing through such circuitous channels, it is nearly impossible for political journalists and activists—no less average citizens—to understand just who is giving money to whom.

Nonpartisan governments offer their own version of opacity, although this consequence of reform is perhaps more intentional than in the case of campaign finance restrictions. Quite simply, we know from a great deal of public opinion research that most voters do not follow politics closely. They have little idea which legislator voted for what bill, calling into question the whole concept of elections as moments of accountability. Parties, however, make such accountability possible. They serve as a convenient cue for voters, allowing them to make informed voting decisions. Voters may not know how their representative voted, but they can tell you whether they are pleased or displeased by the direction of public policy, and if they're displeased, they can vote the current party out of office. This is simply not possible in a nonpartisan election. Not only do nonpartisan elections feature lower turnout than partisan ones (Schaffner, Streb, and Wright 2001), but those voters who do show up in nonpartisan elections are generally casting a less informed vote. Other evidence suggests that nonpartisan elections tend to favor Republican candidates more than partisan ones do (Welch and Bledsoe 1986).

Even the direct primary, now a cherished feature of American political life, has had its own drawbacks, adding to the candidates' campaigning costs and to the government's election costs. This is certainly not to suggest that the primary or other reforms are entirely lacking in merit; reformers often bring the best intentions to the policy changes they pursue. And in many cases, they are identifying serious maladies. Excessive partisanship can actually prevent government action on urgent matters. Massive campaign spending contributes to public mistrust of government and may enhance existing representational inequalities. But more often than not, such reforms only temporarily slow the pathologies they seek to cure. And sometimes, like the remedy that is worse than the cure, they create an environment more toxic to democracy than curative.

Throughout this book, I attempt to point out the electoral consequences of particular reforms, allowing the reader to assess the intended effect of the reform, the actual effect on parties, and the unanticipated effect on democracy in general.

THE PLAN OF THE BOOK

Unlike most books on the relationship between parties and elected officials in the United States, this one does not focus on the American presidency or the Congress. Rather, I turn my focus largely to the states. State research offers us a chance to observe the effects of a much wider range of institutional changes than the national government has ever experienced, albeit within a framework similar to that laid out by the US Constitution and involving individuals who are still very much Americans. The idea of states as "laboratories of democracy" has a double meaning for political scientists. Not only do the states experiment with policies that may later be adopted by the federal government, but the states also allow us to test hypotheses about representative democracy in a way that just focusing on the federal government does not.

Moreover, focusing on the states allows us to examine some 50 different party systems rather than one national one. This is very useful from a scientific perspective given how little we still know about parties. Indeed, political scientists still do not have a commonly accepted definition of a political party. What better way to figure out what parties are than to take a sample of them and subject them to various stresses and stimuli? This is precisely what the states have done, taking structures that are broadly similar across states lines but imposing experiments on them. Through an examination of some of these "natural" experiments, this book aims to provide a more complete picture of just what parties are.

The cases I have selected are all states in which the Progressive movement of the early 20th century was strong. The states—California, Colorado, Minnesota, Nebraska, and Wisconsin—produced some of the leading Progressive politician-philosophers, including Robert La Follette, George Norris, and Hiram Johnson, and saw Progressives capture at least partial control of their governments. I have selected these states because they attempted some of the most dramatic antiparty reforms in American history. I do not suggest that their experiences are typical of American states. Rather, I argue that these experiences allow us to see how parties function under extreme circumstances—when their funds have been cut off, when their powers have been sharply curtailed, or even when they have been formally banned—giving us insight into their composition and behavior.

Chapter 2 provides some further theoretical discussion of the problem at hand, offering more concrete definitions of the concepts of party and reform. I review the fascinating history of the adoption of the direct primary across much of the nation in the early 20th century and note how that reform ultimately failed to deliver on the promises of its proponents. Chapter 3 is the first of the empirical chapters, examining an interesting development at the state level in response to campaign finance reform. Colorado's political parties faced a two-pronged attack in

2002 when the Bipartisan Campaign Reform Act (BCRA, also known as McCain-Feingold) and a state constitutional initiative suddenly restricted their ability to fund their preferred state and federal candidates for office. An enterprising group of wealthy liberal activists, however, helped guide the state's Democratic Party around these impediments. Working in concert with Democratic leaders both inside and outside the statehouse, Colorado's "Gang of Four" targeted races, recruited candidates, developed campaign strategies, and channeled millions of dollars to key Democratic statehouse candidates. In effect, when one portion of the party network was constrained, another activated to compensate, ensuring continued support for candidates in need. This work not only changed the face and function of the party, but also gave that party a competitive edge, helping Democrats take over both chambers of the statehouse the same year that George Bush beat John Kerry by a five point margin statewide.

Chapter 4 focuses on Nebraska's experience with nonpartisanship. Nebraska has enjoyed a fully nonpartisan, unicameral legislature since the mid-1930s, and studies suggest that the legislators themselves are extremely happy with the system even while partisan activists outside the government want it changed. Interestingly, while the chamber's voting patterns remained depolarized and disorganized for decades, they have started to polarize in recent years. Indeed, Nebraska has polarized more quickly in the past decade than any other state. Some new evidence suggests that term limits, which came late to Nebraska, have provided policy demanders with a new way to access political power. By involving themselves in the recruitment of new legislators, activists have been able to install a more partisan brand of incumbent into the capitol.

Chapter 5 looks at another state's experience with a nonpartisan legislature. Unlike in Nebraska, the Minnesota statehouse went nonpartisan at the behest of legislators, rather than voters. The chamber adopted nonpartisanship almost inadvertently in 1913 as part of a miscalculated legislative gambit, although the system was quickly embraced by the public and remained in effect for 60 years. That the legislature itself voted to return to partisanship in 1973, at the same time that parties were coming under increased scrutiny across the country, is notable. Events in Minnesota point to the importance of parties to the legislators themselves: they had formed themselves into Liberal and Conservative caucuses and regularly participated in partisan events long before parties officially returned. The move toward chamber partisanship appears to have come from innovative policy demanders outside the legislature—labor unions and business groups—who formed alliances with Liberal and Conservative legislators, respectively, and compelled them to vote with their parties, even if voters never saw party labels.

The sixth chapter looks at parties' responses to another type of nonpartisan election. Under rules passed by the Progressives in the early 1910s, California allows for the recall of elected officials, but the election to replace a removed official is conducted in a nonpartisan fashion. As the 2003 recall of Governor Gray Davis showed, this has important consequences: the replacement ballot contained 135 candidates, including a variety of mid-tier entertainers, celebrities, and politicians. It was a potentially chaotic election, and observers warned that the winner could take office with as little as 10 percent of the popular vote. Activists in both parties, however, played a crucial role in structuring the campaigns, advantaging a few candidates and pushing others out of the race through a combination of donations, endorsements, and bullying. As a result of all this maneuvering, the election results looked surprisingly conventional, with three candidates capturing 94 percent of the vote and the winner taking office with 49 percent of all ballots cast.

Chapter 7 is a study of one of the first antiparty reforms attempted by the Progressives: the direct primary in Wisconsin. This device was hailed by Progressives like Robert La Follette as a way to disempower party leaders and their corporate benefactors by transferring the power of nominating candidates for office from a few hundred convention delegates to thousands of voters. Yet an analysis of voting behavior within the Wisconsin legislators around the time the direct primary was adopted finds that legislators actually became *more* partisan once voters were in charge of their nomination. The parties became stronger and legislators became less representative of their districts under the direct primary. All this points to the power of party leaders to manipulate events even when voters are ostensibly in charge.

The concluding chapter is a discussion of the costs of these reforms for democratic governance, as described above. I attempt to assess the ways these reforms have made elections more challenging for voters and have made governmental processes more obscure and opaque for observers. While a number of excellent political science studies conclude with recommendations for reform, my goals are far less ambitious. I conclude by urging reformers to simply stop reforming, at least for a while.

I employ a variety of methods in each of these studies, interviewing party leaders and officeholders, quantitatively analyzing roll call votes and campaign donations, combing through historical primary sources materials, and mapping the social networks of party actors. The study of party behavior is necessarily a complex one, involving the examination of people who are not always eager to associate themselves with a party or admit to collusion. I do not expect the reader to be persuaded by any one piece of evidence. The preponderance of evidence, gathered from different perspectives and methods, however, tends to favor the arguments this book promotes: that parties are coalitions of creative and intense policy demanders, that they are endemic and essential to democratic politics rather than disruptive of it, and that attempts to rein in or eliminate them are inherently futile and undermine the goals of accountability and transparency that their proponents purport to seek.

2

Parties and Reforms

The subsequent chapters of this book provide numerous examples of what is essentially the same story: a party adapting to a reform. That simple phrase, however, contains two key concepts—party and reform—that are surprisingly elusive in their definitions. Without some clear idea of just what these terms mean, the rest of the book is simply a collection of disconnected, if occasionally amusing, anecdotes about state politics. In this chapter, I define the key concepts, which have become the source of considerable debate among scholars. I begin with what is easily the more controversial one: party.

PARTY

Political scientists who study, say, Congress, elections, or Japan, while facing no shortage of methodological and conceptual challenges, at least have the luxury of agreeing on what they're studying. Party scholars, conversely, spend an inordinate amount of time disagreeing about what exactly it is they're researching. Party scholars have been likened to blind people describing an elephant, each relying solely on their sense of touch as applied to different parts of the beast (Cohen et al. 2008). There seems to be broad agreement that Burke's ([1790] 1973) idea of a party as a group of men united by common principle is incorrect. (Were the Democrats of the 1950s united on a broad range of issues? If not, did that make them any less of a party?) But what's the right answer?

A number of approaches to the study of parties focus on legislative coalitions. It is not that they ignore other aspects of parties (party organizations, voter loyalties, etc.), but rather that they suggest that the beginning of parties lies within the legislature. This is where public priorities are debated at an elite level and where those with differing views vie for power, usually by contesting elections. What begins as a policy argument among elected officials ends up involving rival candidates, party staff, activists, donors, and, eventually, voters.

One of the dominant approaches within this framework derives from an unpublished manuscript by Thomas Schwartz (1989) and John Aldrich's famous book *Why Parties?* (1995). These works nicely lay out the logic for officeholders to band together in parties. Quite simply, a partyless legislature is a collective action nightmare. Having to cobble together a winning coalition on every bill one cares about is nearly impossible, ensuring that incumbents will fail to enact much of the agenda on which they ran for office and will fail to deliver redistributive benefits to their district. This will disappoint their constituents, who will be disinclined to send the incumbents back to the capitol in the next election.

A party, defined as a stable coalition on a broad range of issues, solves these problems. Incumbents no longer need to assemble winning majorities on each vote for each bill—just by being a part of the larger coalition, they are assured of a very high probability that their priorities will pass. This will help endear them to their constituents, who will respond by providing the incumbents with long, stable careers. Being in the minority party in such a system is, of course, worse than being in a nonpartisan system, since you are virtually guaranteed to win nothing and to have your constituents plundered for resources that are redistributed to the winning coalition's voters. Those who are in the minority, however, still recognize the value of party; if they can mobilize enough voters, they can be assured of majority status and the chance to pass their own priorities and redistribute benefits to their own constituents.

As Aldrich (1995, 4) famously claims, a party is an "endogenous institution" that is "the creature of the politicians." Parties are thus of tremendous value to politicians, enhancing their abilities to succeed in
one legislative session and remain there for subsequent ones. Politicians
should thus desire political parties, seek to protect them when they are
endangered, and build them when they are weak or absent. Arguably, this
is what occurred in the early United States Congress. Initially a partyless chamber, its members soon polarized around questions of the scope
and power of the national government. When the minority Jeffersonians
became annoyed that they were consistently losing legislative battles to
the majority Hamiltonians, they organized local campaign clubs and networks and eventually won majority control. The Hamilton faction then
countermobilized, resulting in a competitive two-party system.

Other examples, however, place great strain on this theory. For example, under a Progressive Era innovation known as cross-filing (1913–59),
California politicians were free to run in as many party primaries as they
wished without their party label appearing next to their name on the ballot. The result of the adoption of cross-filing was a dramatic drop in legislative partisanship. Interestingly, oral histories and roll-call records suggest
that not only did legislators tolerate this weakly partisan system quite
well, they actually protected it. They had a choice between programmatic
government and an easy legislative life devoid of acrimony and repeatedly
chose the latter (Masket 2009b). As I explain in chapter 4, Nebraska has
largely followed that same path since the advent of its nonpartisan legislature in 1937, at least until recently. Arguably, the former Confederate
states survived with relatively nonpartisan politics for roughly a century
(Key 1949). And members of Congress have persistently resisted committee reforms designed to make their legislature more programmatic and
productive, instead preserving their positions of authority to aid in their
own reelection prospects (Adler 2002).

In numerous cases, as it turns out, politicians appear to not have
much of a problem with weak or nonexistent parties, and indeed they
seem to prefer weak parties to strong ones. Why would this be the case?
The answer is that politicians are not the only components of parties,

even if they are very important ones. Parties also consist of a broad range of actors who are interested in doing things other than winning and holding office. They want the government to do something—to move in some direction, to raise or lower taxes, to extend or rescind rights and regulations, to draw or erase moral distinctions, and so forth. These actors, including activists, benefit seekers, lobbyists, and others, are what Cohen and colleagues (2008) refer to as "intense policy demanders" (see also Bawn et al. 2012; Beck 1997), and the logic of the minimal winning coalition is just as relevant to them as it is to officeholders and office-seekers. Policy demanders will often agree with politicians within their party on a broad range of issues, but they occasionally disagree on some important tactical issues with regards to party.

How do these intense policy demanders get the government to do what they want it to do? Incumbent legislators, after all, have a very useful tool for enforcing their decisions: the legislative caucus (Cox 1987; Cox and McCubbins 1993; 2005). They can use their caucus in a cartel-like fashion to ensure that only bills favored by a majority of the majority party even make it to the floor for a vote. Thus, passage votes rarely have surprising outcomes. But by what means may a party of intense policy demanders outside the government push its agenda? Schattschneider (1942) answered this question years ago in his book *Party Government*: They form a united front to control nominations. By serving as the gatekeepers to office, they ensure that only those politicians who support the coalition's views and agenda will ever hold power (Kent 1924). As Schattschneider explained (1942, 64), whoever determines a party's nominees runs the party:

> If [the nomination] is binding, if all other candidates within the party (for the office in question) are denied party support, and if the party is able to concentrate its strength behind the designated candidate, a nomination has been made *regardless of the process by which it is made*. . . . He who can make the nominations is the owner of the party. (Emphasis in original.)

That is to say, those in charge of the party do not need to be formal party staffers or incumbents or anyone else specifically. Whoever can credibly claim to have determined a nomination, be it a legislative caucus or the attendees at a convention or a shadowy group of business elites, *is* the party for all intents and purposes. Recognizing this aspect of parties is key to understanding their flexibility and their resilience to reform.

Importantly, when these policy demanders conspire to control nominations in the United States, they largely do so without the benefit of formal institutional structures. Rather, they rely on social networks. As some recent research has shown, officeholders, candidates, formal party organizations, periodicals, activists, and others often work together toward common ideological goals, sharing information and campaign resources to form the outline of a party network (Bernstein 1999; Doherty 2006; Koger, Masket, and Noel 2009; 2010). These party networks can be observed advantaging preferred candidates for federal offices (Dominguez 2005; Noel 2011) as well as candidates at the state and local level (Masket 2009b; 2013a). The network, of course, is a remarkably resilient structure, capable of adapting to institutional changes and to the loss or addition of actors. As I demonstrate in subsequent chapters, party networks have successfully circumnavigated some antiparty reforms that tend to treat parties as static, monolithic institutions.

When these intense policy demanders gather together to pick the candidates they like and install them in office, they certainly satisfy Anthony Downs's (1957) definition of a party as "a coalition of men seeking to control the governing apparatus by legal means." What's more, as a response to this, a party system will soon evolve: "Some initially inactive citizens will be directly hurt or angered by policies of the first party, become active as intense policy demanders, and form an opposition party" (Cohen et al. 2008, 35–36).

This view of parties as networks of policy demanders is something of a departure from previous research that focused on the group basis of parties. Epstein's (1967) pluralist model of parties saw them as representing the diverse array of interests that comprise the American political landscape, while Key (1952) acknowledged organized pressure groups as the main drivers of American political institutional behavior. The current arrangement of America's political parties may well be captured by Sartori's (1976) concept of "polarized pluralism." These and other political scientists viewed parties as being strongly driven by their constituent interest groups, but did not necessarily see the ties between all these policy demanders as the party in itself.

Seeing parties as networks of policy demanders rather than just politicians isn't necessarily a refutation of Aldrich's description of parties as the creatures of politicians. After all, Aldrich also describes a party as "an institutionalized coalition . . . of elites" that has "adopted rules, norms, and procedures" in order to "capture and use political office" (1995, 283–84). I view this as more of an expansion of Aldrich's definition. Parties may certainly come as the result of legislative maneuvering by incumbent politicians. Arguably, legislative leaders like former California Assembly Speaker Jesse Unruh (D) or former US House Speaker Newt Gingrich (R) built up party organizations from within their respective legislative chambers. But sometimes—indeed, quite often—politicians themselves are reticent to employ such tactics, and it is the policy demanders who insist on partisanship.

It is an empirical question, albeit a difficult one, whether parties are built more often or more effectively outside the government or inside it, or whether the legislative caucus or the united front in nominations is the better tool for party creation and maintenance. Making the question even more challenging to answer is the fact that different observers may see the same incidence of party genesis and draw different conclusions. Aldrich (1995) and Schattschneider (1942), for example, depict the emergence of parties in the United States as resulting from disagreements in the early US Congress, as described earlier. Cohen and colleagues (2008), however, look at the same events and detect the hand of intense policy demanders outside the Capitol. Democratic clubs, preaching the philosophies of Jefferson, began organizing in Philadelphia in 1793 and then spread to other cities throughout the nation, organizing criticism of Federalist policies. Their activities were abetted by newspapers, the writers and editors of which had begun their careers as anti-Federalist activists. Later clubs played a role in disseminating campaign literature and ballots and served as a training ground for new candidates for office. The authors additionally make the provocative argument that the Founders themselves were a political party of sorts, building a government to advance their interests and protect those interests from the "undue influence" of those with different priorities.

These accounts need not be mutually exclusive. Politicians and policy demanders may work simultaneously both inside and outside the government to create or strengthen a party system. This book, however, argues that such activities tend more often to come from outside the government for the very simple reason that incumbents have more to gain (or less to lose) from a nonpartisan system than activists do. As much empirical evidence will attest, incumbents can still enjoy lengthy and prosperous careers in the absence of parties. It is a rare activist that can secure her policy goals in such a system.

Other studies have found that parties are not always operating in service of their incumbents, but rather pursuing their own agendas regardless of what their incumbents want. Galvin (2012), for example, finds evidence that the national parties did not, *contra* Aldrich, suddenly become organizations lying in service to candidates in the 1960s. Rather, Galvin argues, the parties built up their capacities asymmetrically and at different times, usually in response to consecutive electoral defeats; the Republicans staffed up their party during the New Deal, and the Democrats did so during the Reagan and Bush administrations in the 1980s. The parties, it seems, have their own agendas, irrespective of what officeholders want, and will respond to environmental threats as they see fit. Recent history finds examples of parties seeking to enhance their ability to punish errant lawmakers (Van Oot 2011) or to force candidates out of competitive primary races (Masket 2011). In such cases, it seems that politicians are the creatures of parties, rather than the other way around (Bawn et al. 2012).

This raises an important concern for scholars: it can be difficult to determine just who is the creature of whom. When members of Congress vote in lockstep with those of their party, is it because they are trying to advance an agenda, or because they have been selected for such behavior by policy demanders who are trying to press their own agenda and because they fear the wrath of those activists should they fail to perform as expected? The agitations of outsiders and the maneuverings of insiders often occur with near simultaneity, making it challenging to determine agency.

Occasionally, though, history affords us a few convenient natural experiments with which to examine these dynamics. In particular, many reforms created during or inspired by the Progressive Era had the effect of separating the interests of politicians inside the government from those of the policy demanders outside it. Progressive reforms in California in the early 1910s, for example, not only allowed politicians to cross-file, as mentioned above, but also established nonpartisan government at the state and municipal level, and erected barriers between the county and state parties (Masket 2009b). Local parties were thus cut out of politics, allowing us to examine the behavior of incumbents in their absence. This book takes advantage of other similar natural experiments in which the incentives of partisan actors outside the government diverged from those inside the government. The results offer a vivid and complex picture of how parties function.

The examples, spanning several different American states in which the Progressive movement of the early 20th century was strong, vary importantly, but some patterns surface. One is that despite substantial evidence of the stability of officeholders' preferences (Poole 2003), politicians' behavior will tend to change depending on whether parties exist and who is running them. That is, when groups of ideologues determine party nominations—whether doing so by recruiting a candidate, manipulating a convention, or influencing primary outcomes through the deployment of campaign resources—officeholders selected through this system will behave in a partisan manner. They will do so because they have been selected for such behavior and because it is in their career interests to do so; incumbents who disappoint their nominators may find themselves facing a well-funded, broadly endorsed challenger in the next primary. Conversely, when partisan actors are (temporarily) prevented by institutional rules from influencing party nominations, legislators will often ignore partisan concerns, instead focusing solely on their general election constituency.

This happens because legislators, as ambitious politicians who wish to keep their jobs, will be most responsive to whoever can most easily remove them from office. The mass constituency of a general election, we know, follows politics only sporadically. The typical general election voter tends to be largely ignorant of politics and inconsistent in her beliefs, which do not generally follow any one party's agenda (Campbell et al. 1960; Delli Carpini and Keeter 1993). Conversely, those who are pivotal in making nominations tend to be highly aware of politics, consistent in their preferences, and strongly ideological (Aldrich 1983; Layman and Carsey 2002; Schlesinger 1991). It follows that when legislators are left under the supervision of the general electorate only, legislative politics will be relatively unstructured, with members voting with their constituencies and adhering to whatever temporary coalitions may suit their reelection needs. When partisan actors can control nominations, legislators will attend to their wishes, meaning that legislative politics will tend to be organized in a partisan fashion, with votes falling along a single ideological dimension.

REFORM

The concept of party reform is an elusive one, as scholars spend a great deal of time examining not only the purpose and effects of a given reform but also the intent of the reformers themselves. Each of these areas is fraught with challenges, as well. Any reform that passes a legislature will have scores of advocates. Which of these truly has claim on the "purpose" of a bill? And if we're trying to figure out the intent of a reform group, do we rely on their public utterances, which were no doubt politically calculated to some extent? Do we try to make some determination of what a group had to gain or lose from a given reform, regardless of what their leaders said? Understanding the effects of a reform is no less challenging, as reforms rarely occur within a vacuum. That is, reforms often pass at a time when there has been a shift in public or elite opinion about policy;

should we ascribe changes to the political system after the reform's passage a result of the reform or a result of the same forces that gave rise to the reform in the first place?

Before even attempting to address such issues, though, we must be clear about what we mean when we talk about a party reform or a reform movement. Traditional interpretations usually see party reformers as seeking to curb the worst abuses of party politics (voter fraud and intimidation, lack of competition, disenfranchisement, undermining voter input, etc.) with sincere, if occasionally misguided, laws. A revisionist view tends to undermine such simplistic interpretations, noting that different actors had various self-interested reasons for supporting or opposing reform. One may similarly view "reform" as just a name given for the coalition currently out of power. They are no more or less scrupulous than the "machine" they oppose and will seek to protect their own status using antidemocratic means once they achieve office.

To make some sense of these differing views of reform, I will describe them in terms of one particularly powerful and enduring party reform movement of the early 20th century: the adoption of direct primaries.[1] This was indeed a dramatic and rapid change in the way America's political parties nominated candidates for office and was seen as one of the crowning achievements of the Progressive movement. In the 1890s, nearly all state parties nominated candidates via conventions (although there were some local variations); by 1915, 28 of 37 non-Southern states had switched to direct primary elections for nearly every public office in the state (Ware 2002).

The traditional view frames this switch as a story of a sincere group of political activists—including journalists, good government advocates, and some politicians—taking advantage of public discontent with machine control and forcing state legislatures to pass direct primary laws. The problem with the party machines, for many of these reformers, was that they were doing the bidding of faceless corporations bent on enriching themselves at the public's expense. The parties of many Western and Midwestern states found themselves under the dominion of transportation and extraction

1. I provide a detailed examination of the effects of this reform in Wisconsin in chapter 7.

industries. For example, as Mowry (1951) writes, the California state legislature at the turn of the 20th century was widely (and mostly accurately) perceived as being under the control of the Southern Pacific Railroad, and the way the railroad company enforced its rule was by being able to hand-pick nominees for the legislature at state conventions of the majority Republican Party. "Scarcely a vote was cast in either house," wrote an observer of the 1907 legislative session in that state, "that did not show some aspect of Southern Pacific ownership, petty vengeance, or legislative blackmail" (quoted in Mowry 1951, 19–20). As long as such corporations controlled party nominations, the state government would be neither accountable nor responsible to the people. Direct primaries were the means to make elected officials responsive to citizens, rather than to the corporate-backed party bosses (Wiebe 1967). As political observer F. M. Brooks remarked in 1897,

> It is the power to nominate which makes the "boss" and the "machine." Bosses cannot control the voters. They control and get their power from delegates, party workers, politicians, office-holders and office-seekers. Take away the power to nominate, and bosses and machines will cease to exist. (Quoted in Ware 2002, 208)

US Senator George W. Norris of Nebraska similarly promised, "The direct primary will lower party responsibility. In its stead it establishes individual responsibility" (quoted in Ranney 1975, 4). Wisconsin Progressive lion Robert La Follette vowed that once party conventions were eliminated, "no longer ... will there stand between the voter and the [elected] official a political machine with a complicated system of caucuses and conventions, by the easy manipulation of which it thwarts the will of the voter" (quoted in Reynolds 2006, 184).[2]

Political observers in the wake of the widespread adoption of direct primaries generally deemed it a success. Political scientist Austin Ranney

---

2. Interestingly, a number of democracies, particularly in Latin America, have begun adopting direct primaries in recent decades with the assumption that such a reform will actually *increase* polarization. Empirical studies, however, suggest no such increase after primaries are adopted (Serra 2011; 2015).

(1975, 6) proclaimed, "The direct primary in most instances has not only eliminated boss control of nominations but party control as well." No less an authority than the US Supreme Court determined that "direct primaries, which have become by far the most common method of selecting party nominees, allow candidates to appeal over the heads of voters. They have become a prime device for weakening party discipline" (*Ray* v. *Blair* 1952).

In this view, the reformers of the early twentieth century are true heroes of American democracy. The local party leaders, either pursuing their own needs or those of their corporate masters, were actively thwarting democratic procedures through their control of party nominations at the conventions. Nomination via direct primary was thus a serious threat to the bosses' power, one they actively opposed. But it was impossible to defeat an idea whose time had come. The collection of Progressive reformers rode a wave of public outrage against machine abuses to enact direct primaries across the country.

Proponents of a more revisionist view of this history, however, note that the traditional account suffers from a serious logical flaw. If party bosses were so powerful as to be able to control an entire legislature of elected officials, how did they lose on what was arguably the most important vote for their continued dominance? And how did they lose in state after state? And just how much of a cudgel could public opinion have been on a question of party nomination procedures? Either the party bosses were not nearly as important or powerful as the traditional view suggests, or the nature of the adoption of the direct primary has been mischaracterized.

The proper interpretation, argues Alan Ware (2002), is more the latter. The direct primary may have presented some challenges for party bosses, but it also solved some significant problems for them. The main problem parties were facing in the late 1800s was one of scale; the country, urban areas in particular, was simply becoming too populous for the kind of face-to-face politics that worked in Andrew Jackson's day. As society became larger and more anonymous, it became more difficult to do things like police party conventions. (Just who were all these delegates, anyway?)

This increased anonymity in political circles gave rise to much more transparent ambition on the part of office seekers. Candidates prior to the 1880s were generally judged poorly if they actively sought a party's nomination. "The individual is nothing," was the credo of the day. "Party, in a true sense, is everything" (Reynolds 2006, 67). A nominee, once chosen, usually did not even speak publicly to convention delegates except to utter a brief word of thanks. Very quickly, that changed, to the point where candidates bragged of seeking nominations. As J. R. McDonald, California's Treasurer, claimed in 1894,

> [E]veryone has known that I am an aspirant for Governor. I have made my canvas in the San Joaquin Valley and the southern portion of the State. In some of the counties I know that entire delegations could not have been elected had they not been pledged to me. (Quoted in Reynolds, 79)

Candidacies soon became less about the party and more about the individual candidate. For example, Republican Party leaders in 1884, writes Klinghard (2010), recognized that they were constraining themselves when they nominated Grover Cleveland for president, as he disagreed with many of them on the Pendleton Civil Service Reform Act. This was a significant departure from past practice:

> The old notion held that the presidential nominee was "available"— capable of representing the widest range of party factions possible— rather than a substantive leader. Cleveland implied the opposite: a party that selected a candidate with a well-known position on an issue came to pledge itself to that issue and so grafted his views onto its official "aura." As the *Seattle Post-Intelligencer* would put it, he was claiming that "he constitutes party opinion, party caucuses, party conventions, party platforms, nay, even the party itself, all within the circumference of one capacious waistband!" (Klinghard 161)

During the 1912 presidential election, a New Jersey politician similarly remarked, "A party platform was hardly necessary for the candidate is a platform in himself. If anyone asks you what the Democratic platform is, just tell him, 'Wilson'" (quoted in Reynolds 2006, 86).

The rise in the number of people actively seeking nominations created a crisis for party leaders. For every person they hand-selected to be the nominee, several others rose up to claim the backing of important segments of the party. Soon, the blessing of the party boss wasn't enough; rival candidates might claim to be the legitimate nominee. It was not unheard of for the same party to nominate different people for the same office in separate conventions (Reynolds 2006, 124). The parties risked fragmenting their vote and tossing the election to their opponents unless they could come up with a way to make a clear claim of just who the nominee was. This was where the state came in, serving as a neutral, final arbiter. Thus the move to primary elections, governed by the state, solved a serious problem confronting party leaders. To be sure, it created others—voters were much harder to control than delegates—but these were not insurmountable.[3]

Direct primaries could also be seen as the means by which candidates (rather than reformers) triumphed over bosses. As the norms governing the open display of candidate ambition changed in the 1880s, officeholders who enjoyed their positions of power came into conflict with party leaders, who often arranged for rotation of offices to allay the influx of ambitious candidates. If a boss could control the nomination, it was largely futile for an officeholder to try to stay in office once asked to leave. By placing the nomination decision in the hands of impressionable voters, however, officeholders had a better chance of remaining in power indefinitely. Illinois governor Charles Deneen, for example, utilized the direct primary to secure his own reelection in 1908, making him the first two-term governor in decades. As one of his rivals charged, "Under this primary law it is practically impossible to defeat the Governor in office for nomination if he uses his office to renominate himself" (Ware 2002, 153). As Reynolds (2006, 197) writes, "Republican and Democratic legislators backed the direct primary because it suited their purposes."

Seen in such a light, party reform looks less like a group of benevolent reformers challenging the entrenched bosses and more like a struggle by

---

3. As a growing body of research attests (Bawn et al. 2012; Cohen et al. 2008; Dominguez 2005; Masket 2009b), modern party leaders are quite skilled at securing the nomination of their preferred candidates through their manipulation of key campaign resources.

some political actors to gain an advantage over another group of political actors. Indeed, this is the subtext of Jessica Trounstine's book *Political Monopolies in American Cities* (Trounstine 2008). Trounstine compares party machines like Mayor Richard Daley's organization in mid-20th-century Chicago to the "reform" organizations that later ran cities like San Jose and San Antonio, and finds little to distinguish them, apart from the demographic characteristics of their supporters. Both types of organizations come to power by championing the needs of underserved communities, and both types, once in power, try to preserve their power through unsavory means, transferring public goods to their core constituencies and limiting the ability of other groups to vote or influence government.

The following chapters largely follow the more revisionist model of party reform, attempting to understand the various motivations of reformers. However, I do acknowledge that the authors and advocates of political reform movements may be quite sincere. Advocates of campaign finance reform, for example, include incumbent politicians who would like to limit the financial resources of their potential challengers, but also activists who experience authentic revulsion when they see the quantity of money raised and spent in elections and are concerned that it creates conflicts of interest and undermines democracy (Franz 2013). In each chapter, I seek to distill the central promises and predictions of each party reform effort and compare them with actual outcomes. To a large extent, though, the distinction between sincere and strategic reformers is irrelevant—any given reform movement contains large quantities of both. To the extent that the reformers are seeking a true change in the power and reach of parties, though, they will almost invariably be frustrated in either the short or long term.

REFORMING A PARTY OF POLICY DEMANDERS

Many political reforms contain the seeds for their own demise. The whole literature of historical institutionalism examines not only the long-term trends that may precede and shape a political reform, but also the way reforms tend to change the political system, producing new alliances that may undermine the original reform (Huber and Stephens 2001; Pierson 2005; Skocpol and Pierson 2002). The failure of Bill Clinton's health-reform efforts, and the successes of Barack Obama's, for example, cannot be understood without knowledge of the unusual private health insurance system that emerged in the United States during and after the Second World War, which made the sort of single-payer system that exists in many other advanced democracies a political impossibility (Hacker 2002). This echoes Schattschneider's (1935) claim that "new policies create a new politics."

Such a dynamic seems particularly troublesome for reforms aimed at political parties. A reform designed to limit or prevent a party's influence on politics might work if a party were a clearly definable and fixed entity. It might work if a party were a legislative coalition that could be torn apart.[4] It also might work if the affected actors were disorganized and politically weak. For example, Progressive Era reforms requiring voters to register in advance of elections dramatically reduced voter turnout—generally at the expense of poorer, less educated, and less engaged citizens—and participation remains at these lower levels a century later.

But if a party is a vague network of creative actors seeking control of the levers of power, and if the reform is simply a means to advantage one vague network over another one, then it's hard to imagine it succeeding in the long or even medium run. These parties are nothing if not inventive. They learn from experience, recalibrating their strategies, tactics, and choices of nominees in light of new evidence (Schlesinger 1984). Erect a barrier to their path to power, and they will probe that barrier for weaknesses until they can overcome it.

In the chapters to come, I will detail numerous cases of party reforms that were undermined and overcome. In some cases, this process required decades of innovation. In particular, changes to the nature of ballots that affect the information to which voters are exposed are difficult to overcome. One of the more extreme examples comes from Nebraska, where a state initiative formally banned parties from the state legislature. But

---

4. Colorado's GAVEL ("Give A Vote to Every Legislator") amendment, passed by voters in 1988, notably banned closed-door, binding legislative caucuses.

those who sought to control state politics eventually utilized term limits as a way back to power; the parties took over the role of recruiting new and more ideological candidates for the high number of open seats. Minnesota experienced decades of nonpartisanship, as well, after the legislature passed a nonpartisan ballot law in the 1910s, but policy demanders eventually found a way to create unofficial party factions within the chamber anyway.

Other reforms with less of an impact on voter information may prove easier to overcome. Colorado's Amendment 27, for example, sharply limited the amount of money parties could donate to their preferred candidates, but liberal policy demanders quickly developed a network of funding organizations to make sure that the candidates they liked received the funding they needed. The party system had adapted to this new reform regime within a single election cycle, although the protagonists relied on a structure of party change that had been occurring nationally for several cycles.

Somewhere in the middle lies California's nonpartisan recall. Since this is a device used so infrequently (there have only been three gubernatorial recall elections in all of US history, although the number of recalls of state legislators is on the rise), it is difficult to assess how long it took parties to adapt to it. Nonetheless, California's own rules allowed for only a very short window for campaigning, one in which both parties played extremely active roles in winnowing candidates.

In all these cases, a powerful group (ideological activists, formal parties, etc.) was initially marginalized while another powerful group (officeholders, demanders of certain policies, etc.) benefited. Yet some time later, the marginalized group found a way to return to power and render the reform weakened or moot. The examples demand a much more fluid and extralegislative conception of political parties than has generally been held by scholars, journalists, reformers, and other political observers. The results suggest that parties can be curbed or eliminated only if we proceed from a rigid and unrealistic definition of what parties are. Taken as they actually exist, parties are adaptive and resilient, and can no more easily be eliminated than can disagreement.

3

"Somebody's Gotta Go"

Campaign Finance in Colorado

> In hindsight, what Colorado Democrats did was as simple as it was
> effective. First, they built a robust network of nonprofit entities to
> replace the Colorado Democratic party, which had been rendered
> obsolete by campaign-finance reform. Second, they raised historic
> amounts of money from large donors to fund these entities. Third,
> they developed a consistent, topical message. Fourth, and most
> important, they put aside their policy differences to focus on the
> common goal of winning elections.
>
> FORMER COLORADO REPRESENTATIVE ROB WITWER (2009)

In 2002, Congress passed, and President Bush signed, the Bipartisan
Campaign Finance Reform Act, also known as McCain-Feingold or BCRA.
One of this bill's major goals was to reduce the influence of "soft money,"
the name given for unregulated spending by political parties on behalf of
candidates. BCRA essentially banned soft money—all party donations to
federal candidates were thenceforth subject to the same restrictions and
reporting requirements as regular "hard" donations from individuals.
This, of course, posed a challenge for the major political parties, which
have often sought to strategically allocate resources by devoting thousands

or even millions of dollars to a handful of candidates in highly competitive races. Strategic allocation of resources was suddenly a great challenge.

That same year, Colorado's voters passed state constitutional amendment 27, which accomplished something similar to BCRA at the state level. The amendment sharply limited what individuals and parties could donate to state legislative candidates. Many political observers and party leaders within the state predicted the swift decline of the state's political parties, if not their death, for want of money. Such predictions proved quite premature, however, as parties quickly adapted to this reform and partisan sources were soon directing more money than ever at their preferred candidates.

Some version of this party adaptation occurred all across the United States over the last decade, as party leaders sought ways to overcome new limits and still exert their influence on elections. This chapter focuses on one particular case, that of Colorado's Democrats, who were among the quickest and most innovative adapters in the country. The path they pursued has been a model for other state parties, and it makes for a useful and revealing case study in how parties overcome a reform designed to constrain them while still staying technically within the boundaries of the law (Schrager and Witwer 2010).

This chapter starts out by describing the double reform that hit Colorado in 2002. I then examine the response by the state's Democrats to these reforms, assessing whether the structures they built up were influential in elections. The results suggest that the Democrats' innovation was an important one, giving their party's elected officials greater control over the state and making the party itself stronger than it had been prior to reform. This, I explain, offers us a useful example of party adaptation, demonstrating how policy demanders are able to adjust to new legal regimes and still secure the kind of partisan behavior they desire from elected officials.

REFORM AND RESPONSE

Compared to federal elections, state legislative elections tend to involve paltry sums of money. The 2010 elections to the US House of Representatives saw

$1.09 billion raised by all the candidates across all 435 districts, averaging $2.5 million raised per seat. Conversely, state legislative candidates in all 7382 state legislative districts that year raised $593 million, coming to an average of just over $80,000 per seat.[1] Given these small sums, a few thousand dollars properly spent can end up making a large difference in state legislative races.

State legislative races also feature a wide range of limitations on campaign spending. In some states, including Alabama, Indiana, and Nebraska, there is no upper limit on what individuals or political parties may donate to state legislative candidates. Other states feature very tight limitations—Montanans may not contribute more than $160 to a candidate for their state legislature.[2] Colorado, in particular, saw a dramatic change in its campaign finance rules starting in 2002, with limitations on campaign donations dropping from typical levels to among the lowest in the nation. Colorado's Amendment 27 prohibited individuals from donating more than $200 to a state legislative candidate,[3] whereas the previous cap had been $1000. Parties, which could previously spend unlimited sums on candidates for state legislative, were now limited to $18,000 for state senate candidates and $13,000 for state house candidates. The amendment also substantially cut into the parties' revenue streams, lowering the limit on individual donations to political parties from $25,000 to $3000 (Legislative Council of the Colorado General Assembly 2002).

Advocates of Amendment 27 claimed that the reform would "reduce the impact of special interests on the political process and increase the influence of individual citizens." Supporters promised that the amendment would also improve transparency by giving "people information about who is paying for these advertisements right before an election" (Legislative Council of the Colorado General Assembly 2002). Despite opposition by the *Denver Post* and the *Rocky Mountain News*, the state's two largest newspapers at the time, Amendment 27 passed by an overwhelming 66–34 margin.

---

1. This average is skewed a bit by the spending patterns of wealthy outlier states, such as California, Texas, and Illinois. The median funds raised per legislative seat were only $48,000.
2. http://www.ncsl.org/Portals/1/documents/legismgt/limits_candidates.pdf.
3. That limit is doubled for candidates who agree to voluntary spending limits of $65,000 for state house candidates and $90,000 for state senate candidates.

These new regulations arrived simultaneously with Congress's passage of BCRA in 2002, which placed limits on donations to federal candidates. Thus state parties were simultaneously stymied in their ability to affect both federal and state races and were incentivized to develop solutions. As a result of these reforms, party leaders wishing to channel funds to preferred candidates in the 2004 races, whether at the state or federal level, had to either abide by these restrictions or come up with some way to get around them.

Many forms of regulation have been subject to the law of unintended consequences, and campaign finance reform is no exception.[4] Since the passage of the Federal Election Campaign Act in 1971, attempts to drive money from elections have seen the level of expenditures only increase. This pattern has manifested itself faithfully in Colorado over the last decade.

In this case, the innovation came not simply from party leaders looking for ways around the law, but from intense policy demanders looking for a way to influence elections and to take control of a political party and a state government. The Colorado example involves a handful of very wealthy liberals who were dissatisfied with the direction their state government was going and thought that things would be considerably better should the statehouse flip to Democratic control. These activists consist of four main individuals, sometimes simply referred to as "the four millionaires" (Steers 2006):

- Tim Gill, the Denver-based founder of Quark software.
- Jared Polis, a Boulder entrepreneur who had helped develop BlueMountain.com and ProFlowers, which he sold for $700 million and $477 million, respectively. In 2008, Polis would be elected to the US Congress, representing Colorado's Second district.
- Pat Stryker, the Fort Collins heiress to a family medical corporation, who has an estimated worth of roughly $1 billion.

---

4. Just because the effects were unintended does not mean that they were unanticipated. The night Amendment 27 passed in 2002, lobbyist Becky Brooks predicted, "Two years from now, all the money will go underground. There won't be any less money in politics. We just won't know where it's all coming from, and the candidates themselves won't have any control over it" (Booth 2002).

- Rutt Bridges, who made a fortune creating land surveying software for petroleum companies and later built a nonprofit organization, the Bighorn Center for Public Policy, with the aim of
  improving public discourse.

Gill and Polis, notably, are gay (although Polis was not publicly so at
the time of these events [Burnett 2006]), and were incensed by Colorado
legislation and initiatives targeting the state's gay and lesbian population.
The narrow passage of Amendment 2 in 1992, which excluded gays and
lesbians from state antidiscrimination laws, was a particular wake-up
call for Gill, who shortly thereafter created a foundation designed to pro-
mote gay rights. The Gill Foundation remained largely unaligned politically, however, until the 2004 state legislature's consideration of House
Bill 1375, which would have prevented school districts "from providing
instruction relating to sexual lifestyles that are alternative to heterosexual
relationships, except in the context of instruction concerning the risk and
prevention of sexually transmitted disease." Gill sat in the audience as
the House Education Committee passed the bill 6–5 on a party-line vote,
with all Republicans voting aye. He left the building telling a friend his
new motto: "Somebody's gotta go" (Schrager and Witwer 2010).

From that point on, these four individuals began closely conspiring to
build a network of 527s with the explicit purpose of putting Democrats
in control of both state houses. The idea was to circumvent campaign
finance laws by having independent expenditure committees amass millions of dollars and channeling that money to a carefully targeted group
of races that would be pivotal for statehouse control. The team would soon
become known as Colorado's "Gang of Four," although they preferred to
call themselves the "Roundtable."

It is important to acknowledge here that the four Roundtable members
were hardly political neophytes—several had political ambitions of their own.
Polis had been an elected member of the Colorado State Board of Education
since 2001, and by 2007 he was running for Congress. Bridges (unsuccess-
fully) ran for governor in 2006. It is also worth noting that the Roundtable
did not operate independently of other party leaders. Its members met

frequently with many top Democrats in Colorado and Washington, DC. Legally, of course, the Roundtable could not directly coordinate activities with the formal Colorado Democratic Party. As Patricia Waak,[5] who was chair of the party during this time, explained in an interview,

> I had never been totally clear on all the things they do because I'm not permitted to coordinate with them. What I've done instead since I've been the chair is to let them know what the party's doing, which is perfectly legal.

Even if Roundtable leaders couldn't directly coordinate such activities with the party, however, there were sufficient prominent Democrats acting as go-betweens to make direct conversations between formal party leaders and 527 leaders unnecessary. Joan FitzGerald and Alice Madden, two of the top-ranking Democrats in the state senate and house, respectively, conferred regularly with Roundtable members. A participant at Roundtable meetings describes some of the other regular attendees:[6]

> Beth Ganz (CO Planned Parenthood) was the executive director of America Votes in 2006. Tony Massaro (Colorado Conservation Voters) was the political director of the national League of Conservation Voters from 2006 to 2010. Brandon Hall (director of one of the legislative 527s and then political director at CO SEIU) was last seen managing Harry Reid's 2010 campaign. Joan FitzGerald was the President of AmericaVotes in 2010.

The participant adds that these regular attendees provided key guidance on the decisions made by the Roundtable:

> The Roundtable was much more than just the four millionaires. They held the purse strings, but the decision-making process involved

5. Interview conducted via telephone on February 8, 2011.
6. The subject preferred to remain anonymous. Interview was conducted via e-mail on February 6, 2011.

organizations with skilled political operatives (Planned Parenthood, Colorado Conservation Voters, and a few others), the major union organizations that traditionally support Democrats (AFL, NEA, SEIU, AFSCME, etc.), and the legislative leadership (via formal or informal involvement/communication).

With this august group of people combined with the four millionaires' impressive resources, the Roundtable set about its task of changing the partisan makeup of the state. In 2004, Republicans controlled 18 seats in the state senate to the Democrats' 17 and the Democrats held 28 seats in the state house to the Republicans' 37. Five more house seats and one more senate seat would allow the Democrats to reach their goal, but it was an elusive one—Democrats hadn't held both chambers since the early 1960s.

The members of the Roundtable believed that they could achieve this goal through asymmetric warfare; they would target a small set of winnable legislative races and overwhelm the opposition with the resources they could muster. They established three 527s—one devoted to house races, one for senate races, and one specifically for voter turnout efforts—and devoted massive personal sums to these organizations and encouraged their allies to do the same. The three 527s ended up raising $3.6 million that year—$2.5 million directly from the original four members of the Roundtable—and devoted it all to a small set of state legislative races. Colorado's Republican Party had actually established its own set of 527s at roughly the same time, but those raised only $845,000 that year (Schrager and Witwer 2010, 77). Each of the Roundtable's 22 targeted races[7] thus experienced an average of $189,000 in campaign expenditures from the three 527s, in addition to activity paid for by traditional party sources and the candidates' own personal fundraising efforts. This is an impressive figure, considering that the median state legislative candidate in Colorado raised just $35,000 two years earlier. Indeed, direct contributions to all Democratic state legislative candidates in 2004

7. Ten house races were targeted, along with four senate races, by the 527s devoted to those two chambers. Coalition for a Better Colorado, the 527 devoted to field organization, expanded the circle slightly to 19 total races.

totaled $3.2 million—slightly less than the Roundtable devoted to just its targeted races.

The outcome of the race is at least suggestive that this strategy paid off—Democrats picked up seven house seats and one senate seat, taking control of both chambers, even while the state voted for George W. Bush over John Kerry by five points. Indeed, Bush beat Kerry in six of the state house districts Democrats took over that day (Schrager and Witwer 2010, 124). Of the 22 targeted races across both chambers, Democrats won 19 of them. Two years later, the Roundtable redoubled its efforts, setting up another three 527s and amassing $4.1 million (45 percent of which was provided directly by Gill, Bridges, and Stryker) to be allocated to a select group of 26 competitive house and senate races.[8] Democrats gained four more house seats and two more senate seats that year, winning 22 of their 26 targeted races.

AN AID TO THE PARTY OR A REPLACEMENT?

To what extent did the organization built by the Roundtable usurp the role of the Colorado Democratic Party? As the discussion above suggested, this was not a group with radically different backgrounds or ideas from those already running the formal party in the early 2000s. Indeed, there was considerable crossover between the Roundtable and the formal party, with prominent Democratic elected officials and union leaders providing strategic guidance to both. The Roundtable, in this sense, was simply providing its own vast resources to help the same sorts of candidates in the same sorts of ways that the formal party would be doing anyway.

In another sense, however, something new was occurring. The impression received during several interviews with state Democratic leaders is that Colorado's political elites increasingly began to see the Roundtable's

---

8. The list of target includes 11 initial house races and five senate races, although the targets were expanded in the final voter turnout efforts.

527s as the locus of Democratic Party activity and the formal party as something of an atavistic relic. Even leaders of the formal Democratic Party acknowledge that something important changed in the middle of the last decade. As former party chair Waak remarked in an interview,

> The party had to re-look at what its function was and how it was going to operate to be the most effective. That's not necessarily a bad thing but it does mean that you've got to change course to some extent.

To test the notion that the locus of party activity was moving away from the formal party and towards the Roundtable, I have collected records of campaign contributions to the Colorado Democratic Party over time. I have also collected records of contributions to the Roundtable 527s. The key test is whether donations made to the Roundtable came at the expense of the formal party.

I investigate this question in Figure 3.1. Here, I have compared donations to the formal party and the 527s in two years, 2002 and 2006. These particular years were chosen partially out of necessity and partially because they make for a good comparison; 2002 was the last year of the prereform

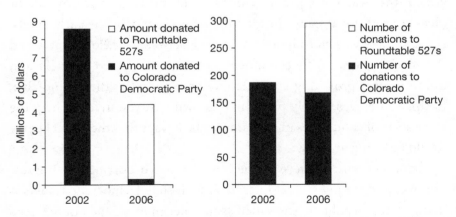

Figure 3.1 Donations to Colorado Democratic Party and Roundtable 527s in 2002 and 2006.
NOTE: Analysis is limited to donations of at least $500. Donation amounts are in current dollars.

system and offers insight into the behavior of political elites before the new contribution limits imposed by Amendment 27 and BCRA. Comparing 2002 to 2004 would make some sense, except that a presidential election is necessarily different from a nonpresidential one, involving considerably more extrastate contributions and presidential-specific funding structures. Furthermore, records of donations to 527s in 2004 are regrettably incomplete. Complete sets of contribution records for 2006, however, do exist, which makes for a better comparison year to 2002 anyway.

The left chart in Figure 3.1 shows the total dollar amount donated to the Colorado Democratic Party (CDP) in 2002 and 2006 and the amount donated to Roundtable 527s. The right chart shows the total number of $500-or-more donations made to these entities in both years. The charts both demonstrate that the CDP saw a decline both in the number of donations and in the total amount of those donations between 2002 and 2006. The CDP received $8.6 million in 2002 but a mere $304,000 four years later, even though the party had gone from minority to majority status in the statehouse at that time and thus theoretically had more to protect and to offer its donors in return. This deficit relative to 2002, however, is partially compensated for by the $4.1 million donated to Roundtable 527s. Additionally, while the number of donations to the CDP was lower in 2006 than in 2002, the total number of contributors to both the Roundtable 527s and the CDP in 2006 was nearly double the number who just gave to the CDP four years earlier.

It should be noted that the 527s' growth is not solely attributable to defections among supporters of the CDP. Indeed, among the 128 people who donated at least $500 to the 527s in 2006, 83 (65 percent) had not given to the party previously. These represent a new donor base, largely cultivated by the Roundtable.

It is telling, however, to examine the donation patterns of the elite donors—those who regularly contribute large sums of money to party entities. Table 3.1 lists the 16 committees and individuals that contributed at least $500 to the CDP in 2002 and also contributed at least $500 in 2006 to either the CDP or one of the Roundtable's 527s. The donors are listed by declining size of their 2002 donation. In parentheses next to each 2006

Table 3.1 DONOR PATTERNS IN 2002 AND 2006

Donor	2002 donation to Colorado Democratic Party	2006 donation to Colorado Democratic Party	(as a percentage of 2002 donation to CDP)	2006 donation to Roundtable 527s	(as a percentage of 2002 donation to CDP)
Democratic Senate Campaign Fund	$3,834,304	$1,804	(0.1)	$0	(0)
House Democratic Majority Fund	$74,259	$1,000	(1.3)	$0	(0)
CO AFL-CIO	$38,500	$1,000	(2.6)	$60,000	(155.8)
United Food & Commercial Workers	$36,500	$3,500	(9.6)	$0	(0)
Democratic Legislative Campaign Committee	$25,000	$0	(0)	$346,884	(1,387.5)
Tim Gill	$25,000	$2,500	(10)	$1,080,000	(4,320.0)
Jefferson County Education Assn.	$25,000	$500	(2.0)	$5,000	(20.0)
Thomas A. Barron	$24,500	$1,000	(4.1)	$0	(0)
CO Building and Construction Trades	$9,500	$1,000	(10.5)	$0	(0)
B. L. Schwartz	$7,500	$2,500	(33.3)	$0	(0)
Communications Workers of America	$5,000	$0	(0)	$2,500	(50.0)
CO Professional Firefighters	$4,500	$2,500	(55.6)	$0	(0)
CO Credit Union	$2,600	$1,200	(46.2)	$0	(0)
CO Legislative Services	$1,500	$0	(0)	$1,000	(66.7)
James Kelly	$1,500	$2,500	(166.7)	$10,000	(666.7)
Ray Kogovsek	$750	$0	(0)	$1,323	(176.4)

NOTE: Table lists all those who donated at least $500 to the Colorado Democratic Party in 2002 and at least $500 in 2006 to either the Colorado Democratic Party or one of the Roundtable's three 527s. Donors are listed in declining order of their 2002 donation. Numbers in parentheses are the donors' 2006 contributions as a percentage of their 2002 contributions to the party.

donation is a figure showing that donation as a percentage of their 2002 donation to the CDP.

As the table shows, all but one of the donors who gave to the CDP in 2002 gave less to the formal party in 2006. The Democratic Senate Campaign Fund, which sent nearly $4 million the CDP's way in 2002, gave less than a thousandth of that in 2006. (There were no US Senate contests in Colorado in 2006.) Several leading union organizations, including the AFL-CIO and the UFCW, drastically reduced their donations to the CDP. Many organizations, including the CWA, gave nothing to the CDP in the latter year. Only James Kelley actually increased his donations to the formal party between the two years.

Many of these same donors who reduced their contributions to the CDP gave substantially more to the Roundtable's 527s. The AFL-CIO gave $60,000 to the 527s, 156 percent of their 2002 donation to the CDP. The Communications Workers of America gave $2,500 to the 527s after zeroing out their contributions to the formal party. The Democratic Legislative Campaign Committee, which in 2002 gave $25,000 to the party, ramped up its donations to $347,000 in 2006, all of which went to 527s.

In all, these elite donors gave less than one percent of their 2002 donations to the CDP in 2006, but gave an average of 37 percent of their 2002 CDP donations to the Roundtable's 527s in 2006. Interestingly, most of the 2006 donations to the CDP did not reach the maximum allowed under the law—donors largely held their donations well under the legal limit and sought to influence elections instead via the Roundtable. Seen in this way, the Roundtable 527s appear to have supplanted a key role of the Colorado Democratic Party, amassing funds and channeling them to candidates in key races.

These funds, incidentally, dwarfed the outside money being spent by other sources. According to the records compiled by the Center for Public Integrity, 19 527s spent $4.5 million in Colorado elections in 2006. The funds spent by the three active Roundtable 527s that year comprised 92 percent of that total.

TESTING EFFECTIVENESS

It seems that the Roundtable's main contributions to Colorado Democratic politics were new donors, a large sum of money, and a way of strategically allocating it. In theory, this is a recipe for campaign success, especially when only one party is attempting it. And the aggregate data certainly suggest it was a successful venture. But it is one thing to note that the Roundtable won the vast majority of its targeted races, and quite another to show that those races were won *because of* the Roundtable's efforts. This section seeks to test the latter claim.

Generally, campaigns might affect the electorate in two distinct ways: by altering voter participation or by persuading voters. Down-ballot races like state legislative contests may be particularly ripe for manipulation of voter turnout. After all, turnout tends to be considerably lower for state legislative races than for congressional races, which in turn tends to be lower than that of presidential contests. Scholars have long noted that voters participate only selectively, often declining to weigh in on low-visibility contests for which they lack sufficient knowledge of the candidates or issues (Bullock and Dunn 1996; Rogers 2013; Wattenberg, McAllister, and Salvanto 2000). Indeed, in 2004, 69 percent of registered Colorado voters turned out to vote for president, but only 66 and 60 percent of them participated in congressional and state legislative races, respectively.

The members of the Roundtable were distinctly aware of this trend. Indeed, as Jared Polis reports, they counted on it:

> These down-ballot races have enormous drop-off from the presidential tally, so there's no doubt about it. By building name recognition in down-ballot races, you can of course win seats that are majority on the other side. It's not even a matter necessarily of convincing Bush voters to go for a Democrat, but it's a matter of convincing our voters to check off all the candidates down the line. (Schrager and Witwer 2010, 75–76)

The election summaries provided by Colorado's secretary of state offer evidence of ballot rolloff, providing statistics on the total number of recorded votes and the total number of existing ballots for each legislative contest. We can thus calculate ballot rolloff as the percentage of all ballots received that were valid votes in the contest. An initial examination supports Polis's claims. While 99.2 percent of all ballots in Colorado contained a valid vote for president in 2004, the average rolloff was 5.1 percent for congressional races, 11.3 percent for state senate races, and 12 percent for state house races. It is certainly conceivable that the additional spending and campaign activity decreased ballot rolloff in races targeted by the Roundtable. This leads to testable hypothesis 1:

Hypothesis 1: Ballot rolloff should be lower in targeted state legislative races than in nontargeted ones, all else being equal.

The second possible outcome involves voter persuasion. It tends to be difficult to find strong evidence of voters being directly influenced by a campaign. Although political psychologists have found impressive effects of campaign stimuli in laboratory settings (Ansolabehere et al. 1994; Ansolabehere and Iyengar 1995), these effects tend to be fleeting, and observations of actual campaigns tend to confirm Berelson, Lazarsfeld, and McPhee's (1954) finding that campaigns do little more than encourage voters to vote the way they were going to anyway, and that they're far more influenced by the fundamentals of the political environment than by any advertisement or speech (Bartels and Zaller 2001; Finkel 1993; Gelman and King 1993; Levitt 1994; Lewis-Beck and Rice 1992; Polsby, Wildavsky, and Hopkins 2008; Rosenstone 1983). Nonetheless, a few studies have suggested that campaign techniques—from high-profile speeches to field organization—may influence voters to change their minds, even if the effects are small and temporary (Shaw 1999; Gerber and Green 2000; 2005; Hillygus and Jackman 2003; Imai 2005; Masket 2009a; Silver 2008). This leads to my second testable hypothesis:

Hypothesis 2: The Democratic share of the two-party vote will be greater in targeted state legislatives races than in nontargeted ones, all else being equal.

ANALYSIS

I first turn to a study of ballot rolloff in state legislative elections in 2004 and 2006. The dependent variable in this case is the percentage of all ballots received that contained valid votes in the state legislative race. The unit of analysis is the state legislative district. This study examines all 65 state house districts plus the half of the 35 senate districts that are up in each election year. Uncontested elections are omitted. My main independent variable, *target*, is a dummy variable that equals one if the Roundtable targeted the race and zero otherwise.

The problem with specifying a variable like *target* is that even if there is a positive correlation between targeting and voter turnout, that is not the same thing as a causal relationship. Targets are not selected at random. Roundtable members could well be targeting the sorts of Democratic candidates who seem likely to do well in elections. Indeed, we wouldn't be very impressed with their political acumen if they did not take electability into account. I thus include a control for candidate quality, which has been shown in many studies to be an important predictor of election outcomes (e.g., Jacobson and Kernell 1981). The *High-quality Democrat in race* variable equals one if the Democratic candidate previously held any elected office and zero otherwise. I have also interacted that variable with the *target* variable. This way, we can determine the separate effects of candidate quality and targeting, and also any combined effect when high-quality candidates are targeted.

I also seek to control for other determinants of ballot rolloff. Campaign expenditures may affect rolloff, with greater expenditures raising awareness of the candidates and increasing the likelihood that voters will cast a vote in that contest. Thus, I have included a measure of the total funds raised by both major party candidates. Since this variable has a highly skewed distribution, I have logged it. Notably, these figures are only for the funds raised directly by the candidate and do not include spending by 527s. Thus the effect of the 527s' activities is largely captured by the *target* variable, while the funds-raised variable separates out the effect of traditional campaign spending.

Roundtable members also likely selected candidates based on how competitive their district was. Spending resources in solidly Democratic or solidly Republican districts would likely be a waste of money, but extra funds in an evenly balanced district could make a difference. Thus I have controlled for *district extremism*, calculated as the absolute difference between the district's Democratic voter registration figure and the median Democratic voter registration for all districts.

The *incumbent* variable is a dummy equaling one if there is an incumbent in the race, on the assumption that voters may be more likely to participate in the race if there is a recognizable name attached to it. I control for year with the *year 2006* variable, on the assumption that ballot rolloff would be higher during the 2004 presidential election year, since there would be many voters only there to weigh in on the presidential contest. On the chance that either more liberal or more conservative districts may be more likely to turn out to vote, I have included the Democratic share of two party-voter registration as a control. I also include two variables measuring the percentage of the district that is Latino and African American, respectively.[9] The results appear in Table 3.2.

The table contains four columns. The first shows the results for all state legislative races across both 2004 and 2006. The second limits the analysis to open-seat races. The third is limited to races with a Democratic incumbent, and the forth is for races with a Republican incumbent. The *incumbent in race* variable is obviously eliminated from columns two, three, and four, as are variables with insufficient variance to produce estimates. (For example, all the Democratic incumbents are, by definition, high quality, so the quality variable is omitted from that analysis.) The N for the subsamples is low, so extreme caution is urged when interpreting those coefficients, but the results are nonetheless presented here for the sake of completeness.

9. All data on districts come from the Colorado secretary of state, with the exception of racial composition, which comes from the office of the Legislative Council of the Colorado General Assembly. Roundtable targets were determined by examining campaign disclosure documents of the three 527s in the 2006 race (Main Street Colorado, Moving Colorado Forward, and Citizens for Colorado). These documents include a field stating which candidates were referred to in the election communication.

Table 3.2 REGRESSION ANALYSIS OF VARIABLES PREDICTING BALLOT ROLLOFF
IN COLORADO STATE LEGISLATIVE ELECTIONS, 2004–6

Variable	All cases	Open seats	Democratic incumbents	Republican incumbents
Target	0.250	−0.630	−2.872*	2.331
	(0.785)	(1.041)	(1.292)	(1.185)
High-quality Democrat in race	−0.142	−4.104***	—	0.648
	(0.777)	(1.120)		(1.685)
Target × high-quality Democrat	−0.710	3.620*	—	—
	(1.064)	(1.709)		
Log of campaign funds raised	−1.140**	−1.482*	−0.177	−2.268**
	(0.396)	(0.617)	(0.778)	(0.771)
District ideological extremism	0.072	−0.027	0.068	−0.204
	(0.042)	(0.077)	(0.111)	(0.304)
Incumbent in race	−0.040	—	—	—
	(0.510)			
Year 2006	−3.081***	−1.899*	−3.582***	−2.760***
	(0.453)	(0.762)	(0.846)	(0.750)
Democratic share of voter registration	0.079*	−0.003	0.017	−0.171
	(0.033)	(0.057)	(0.108)	(0.282)
Percentage Latino	−0.023	0.027	0.015	-0.030
	(0.028)	(0.058)	(0.041)	(0.070)
Percentage African American	0.122*	0.343*	0.068	0.151
	(0.055)	(0.138)	(0.090)	(0.095)
Constant	16.433***	23.447**	10.096	39.796*
	(4.585)	(6.932)	(10.914)	(15.613)
Observations	129	45	42	42
	.527	.569	.658	.544

*** $p \le 0.001$, ** $p \le 0.01$, * $p \le 0.05$.

Cell entries left blank where there was insufficient variance to produce coefficients.

NOTE: Ballot rolloff is calculated as the percentage of all ballots received in a district that were valid votes in the state legislative race. Cell entries are ordinary least squares regression coefficients. Standard errors appear in parentheses.

As the results in the leftmost column show, there is no relationship between Roundtable targeting and ballot rolloff for the overall sample. The coefficient for targets is actually positive, though also small and statistically insignificant. Only in the case of Democratic incumbents does Roundtable targeting contribute to lower ballot rolloff, although it is not clear why this would be the case. Incumbency doesn't seem to affect turnout, either. Spending does seem to matter, with a one-point increase in the log of funds raised associated with more than a 1 percentage point decline in rolloff.

The difference between years shows up as statistically significant, with ballot rolloff turning out to be 1.9 to 3.5 points higher in the presidential election. We see relationships with other variables as well, with more liberal and more African-American districts associated with higher rolloff. The overall findings here are generally consistent with expectations but lead to a rejection of Hypothesis 1. Targeting by the Roundtable does not appear to have improved participation in state legislative races.

The next part of the analysis looks at voter persuasion. For this analysis, the dependent variable is the Democratic share of the two-party vote. The independent variables seen in Table 3.2 remain, although with a minor modifications. The *incumbent* variable has been rescaled in the Democratic direction, with Democratic incumbents receiving a value of 1, Republican incumbents receiving a –1, and races with no incumbents getting a zero.

As Table 3.3 shows, Roundtable targets saw a disproportionately greater share of the Democratic vote, a result that is statistically significant ($p \leq .01$). Targeted Democratic candidates received, on average, 3.5 additional percentage points of the two-party vote. This is an impressively large figure—more than twice the calculated incumbency advantage of 1.3 percentage points. The coefficient for Democratic voter registration is unsurprisingly positive and statistically significant, as is that of Democratic fundraising. Neither the candidate quality coefficient nor that of the interaction of quality and targeting reach levels of statistical significance.

The coefficients for percent African American and percent Latino are curiously negative (and the latter is statistically significant). However,

Table 3.3 REGRESSION ANALYSIS OF VARIABLES PREDICTING DEMOCRATIC
SHARE OF TWO-PARTY VOTE IN COLORADO STATE LEGISLATIVE
ELECTIONS, 2004–6

	All cases	Open seats	Democratic incumbents	Republican incumbents
Target	3.471**	2.239	1.082	4.409*
	(1.267)	(2.226)	(1.926)	(1.672)
Democratic share of funds raised	0.125***	0.098*	0.109	0.135***
	(0.023)	(0.043)	(0.064)	(0.031)
Incumbent in race (coded in Dem. direction)	1.325	—	—	—
	(0.741)			
High-quality Democrat in race	0.373	-0.000	—	−2.544
	(1.494)	(2.308)		(2.199)
Target × high-quality Democrat	−2.147	−1.501	—	—
	(1.709)	(3.521)		
District extremism	0.066	−0.138	0.534**	−0.041
	(0.066)	(0.159)	(0.183)	(0.408)
Year 2006	1.300	1.881	1.542	1.204
	(0.717)	(1.513)	(1.330)	(0.964)
Democratic share of voter registration	0.883***	0.915***	0.491**	0.823*
	(0.062)	(0.120)	(0.164)	(0.379)
Percentage Latino	−0.248***	−0.291**	−0.216**	−0.440***
	(0.044)	(0.092)	(0.062)	(0.096)
Percentage African American	−0.099	−0.418	0.052	0.024
	(0.086)	(0.265)	(0.128)	(0.126)
Constant	6.397**	10.019*	24.804*	9.577
	(2.216)	(4.282)	(9.453)	(17.522)
Observations	132	46	44	42
R-squared	.922	.898	.819	.914

*** $p \leq 0.001$, ** $p \leq 0.01$, * $p \leq 0.05$.

Cell entries left blank where there was insufficient variance to produce coefficients.

NOTE: Cell entries are ordinary least squares regression coefficients. Standard errors appear in parentheses.

those coefficients are positive when Democratic voter registration is not included in the equation. In other words, highly black or Latino districts vote Democratic, but somewhat less Democratic than we would expect given voter registration alone.

The results for the targeting variable hold in the case of races involving Republican incumbents, where Roundtable efforts are associated with a 4.4 percentage point increase in the Democratic vote share. The coefficients in open-seat races and races with Democratic incumbents, while positive, fall short of statistical significance, although again the reader should be mindful of the small sample size.

The impact of targeting on the Democratic vote share can be seen graphically in Figure 3.2. This scatterplot shows the Democratic share of two-party voter registration on the horizontal axis and the Democratic vote share on the vertical axis for each contested legislative district in 2004 and 2006. The Roundtable targets are depicted with solid dots. The trendline shows the overall relationship between voter registration and vote share. As can be seen, the vast majority of targeted districts saw Democratic vote shares well in excess of the trendline and above 50 percent.

Finally, Table 3.4 attempts to assess just how much this vote boost mattered. It is a list of all the Democratic state legislative candidates who won

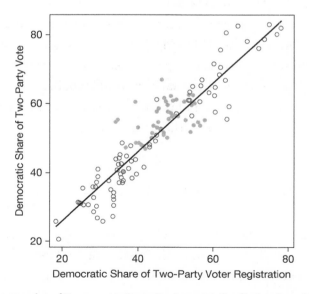

Figure 3.2 Scatterplot of Democratic Party Registration Predicting State Legislative Vote Share, 2004–6.
NOTE: Data points are Colorado state legislative districts in 2004 and 2006. Solid dots indicate districts that were targeted by Roundtable 527s.

Table 3.4 COLORADO DEMOCRATIC CANDIDATES
WHO WON BY LESS THAN ESTIMATED ROUNDTABLE
EFFECT, 2004–6

Year	District	Democratic share of two-party vote	Democratic candidate
2004	HD23	50.1	Green
2004	HD31	51.7	Solano
2004	HD47	51.8	McFayden
2004	HD50	53.1	Riesberg
2006	SD5	51.0	Schwartz
2006	HD27	50.2	Gagliardi
2006	HD29	52.8	Benefield
2006	HD33	51.4	Primavera
2006	HD38	53.1	Rice

their races by less than the estimated vote boost of 3.47 points in 2004 and 2006. All of the Democratic candidates in this category, as it turns out, were targeted by the Roundtable. The implication is that, if not for the influence of the Roundtable, these races would have been won by Republicans. In particular, the table shows that in 2004, four Democratic state house candidates won by margins less than the Roundtable effect. Given that Democrats needed to flip five state house seats to take over the chamber and were only able to flip six, it seems reasonable to say that the Roundtable's activities were pivotal here. Had it not been for the 527s created by the Roundtable, Colorado's state legislature would have remained under Republican control after the 2004 election.

DISCUSSION: IS THIS SOMETHING NEW?

In overcoming campaign finance reform, Colorado's Democrats appear to have fundamentally transformed their party. Several jobs of great importance for a party—recruitment, fundraising, targeting—have, at least to some extent, been outsourced to a small group of wealthy policy demanders. If, as Schattschneider (1942) says, those who make the nominations are the party, is the Roundtable now the Democratic Party of Colorado?

To some extent, this is what its leaders are arguing. Rep. Jared Polis, one of the founders of the Roundtable, argues that this new form of party is actually more efficient and effective than traditional parties are. Traditional party leaders, he argues,

> were selected because they travel the state. They know people. They show up at every dinner. People like them. They manage the palace intrigues effectively. [But] there's no reason to think [party leaders] would be good at running campaigns and making tough decisions.... In fact, to the contrary. They would have a tendency to put valuable resources into races they're probably not going to win because they want to win friends. So, if they like so and so and they're running in a very Republican district, they're going to give them help, which takes it away from a very competitive district. So it wasn't a very good way to allocate resources. (Schrager and Witwer 2010, 68–69)

Founder Tim Gill, meanwhile, even appears to be franchising the organizational style by attempting to bring Democratic control to legislatures in other states where antigay legislation has done well.

So does a new business-savvy elite now function as the state's Democratic Party? Such a claim seems inaccurate, or at least substantially premature. Formal party leaders remain heavily involved with all the key tasks of politicking. The party chair, along with legislative leaders and the heads of various allied interest groups, are still active in the vital activity of candidate recruitment. Indeed, given their familiarity with local leaders across the state (a feature that Polis derides), they are probably still in the best position to hear about up-and-coming politicians and to assess their skills. And while the formal state party is obviously limited in its ability to donate to preferred candidates, it is still one of the major players in this field.

Indeed, if what happened between 2002 and 2006 amounted to a takeover of a party by an external force, we would expect to see this manifested in primary challenges, with different groups backing different sets of candidates in primaries, caucuses, and conventions. Yet such intraparty skirmishes are almost completely absent from this story. The main four members of the Roundtable have been involved in only a handful of primary contests over the past decade, and most of those were basically uncontested.

Figure 3.3 displays the total numbers of contested state legislative primaries by party between 2000 and 2010. In 2004, for example, the first year of the Roundtable's existence, the Democratic Party only saw five contested primaries across 84 state legislative districts, and this was actually down slightly from the numbers in 2000 and 2002. One might expect that the emergence of what are essentially moneyed upstarts in Democratic politics might engender some sort of pushback from earlier party elites or from the formal party leaders. Yet this doesn't appear to have happened.

A possible explanation for this lack of apparent intraparty strife is that Roundtable-backed candidates are deterring the entry of other Democratic candidates through early and ample funding. Interviews failed to uncover much evidence of this occurring, however. A more likely story is that Roundtable leaders and other traditional party leaders are simply converging on the same candidates. For one thing, as explained

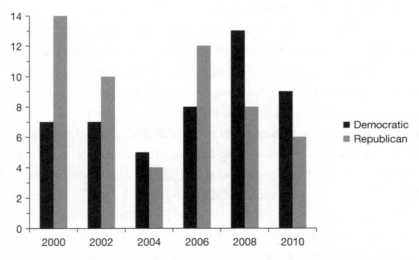

Figure 3.3 Number of Contested Primaries in Colorado State Legislative Races, 2000–2010.
NOTE: Yearly tallies above include contests for the state's 65 state house districts and half of the state's 35 state senate districts.

above, Roundtable leaders and prominent state Democrats are in regular contact with each other and would be able to coordinate their recruiting efforts. For another, sometimes it is simply obvious to all players who the best candidate is. Finally, even if there is disagreement about who the best candidate is, there may simply be little competition for the job. There are only about 875,000 registered active Democrats across Colorado's 65 state house districts—roughly 13,500 Democrats per district. The number of people in each district interested in running for a term-limited, $30,000-per-year job who can take time away from their regular jobs to run for the office and serve in it full-time for 120 days of the year is not large.

It seems clear, then, that the events of 2002–6 did not constitute a hostile takeover of the Colorado Democratic Party. Yet the Roundtable's 527s still seem like something more than just a new campaign device. After all, it is not something that an individual campaign can employ by itself. This can only be done on a large scale, involving a collection of races, a massive amount of funding, and a strategy for allocating it.

What seems to have happened in Colorado is a form of party adaptation. The members of the Roundtable are best thought of as part of the state's Democratic Party network, of no greater or lesser value than the formal party. Through ample funding and clever deployment of those funds, Colorado Democrats have adjusted to the limits imposed by campaign finance reform and even circumvented them. Even more, by adapting to the external shock of reform more quickly than the Republicans, the Democrats were able to secure a campaigning advantage. Their new activities affected enough state legislative elections to flip control of the state house to Democratic even while the state's voters preferred the Republicans' presidential ticket by 5 percentage points.

Have the Republicans caught up to the Democrats in Colorado? Evidence from the 2010 and 2012 elections suggests that they haven't. While Colorado was not shielded from the Republican wave that swept the country that November—the GOP managed to take over the state house in 2010 by a single seat—Republicans fell short on the hotly contested races for governor and US Senate, and Democrats again regained unified control of the government in 2012. At least in part, this appears to be due to an effective network of campaign expenditures. As a *Denver Post* analysis of the 2010 election cycle concluded,

> Colorado's version of liberal super PACs spent nearly 150 times more money than their Republican counterparts in the last election cycle, with most of the money coming from a small circle of unions, wealthy individuals and advocacy organizations. (Crummy 2012)

Roundtable members were involved with intense, well-financed advertising campaigns against US Senate Republican nominee Ken Buck in the 2010 general election and against former US Rep. Scott McInnis in the Republican nomination contest for governor. Both candidates ended up losing those contests narrowly; the gubernatorial nomination went to the little-known Dan Maes, prompting former US Rep. Tom Tancredo to enter the race as an alternative, splitting the Republican vote and handing the race to Democrat John Hickenlooper. To be sure, the Tea Party insurgency played no small part in these Republican losses, but, according to Buck, Roundtable-style funding had something to do with it:

> Why did the Republican wave go over Colorado? . . . I think a lot of it has to do with the fact the Democrats have figured out the party base had to be outside the party, outside the campaign and Republicans are still trying to do it inside the party. [Democrats are] very good at coordinating what appears to be an uncoordinated attack. It worked on me. (Schrager and Witwer 2010, 214)

Even if the parties have reached a level of parity in fundraising capabilities, it is difficult to know this for certain. The increasing complexity of outside funding, involving a rapidly rising number of 527s affiliated with the formal parties, makes it nearly impossible to determine just who is supporting which candidates. As in other states, the adaptation to party reform has made observation of party activities far more challenging. Yet Colorado has provided us of an example of how policy demanders are able to sustain parties even in the face of daunting institutional rules.

4

Polarization without Parties

Nebraska and the Nonpartisan Legislature

In the last chapter, I examined a state in which the parties' abilities to fund their preferred candidates were severely curtailed. This surely created a burden for the parties—one which they creatively overcame—but it was hardly a devastating reform. The parties could still be active in elections and influential about the sorts of people who would populate the legislature and the stances they could take when they got there. But how would parties adapt to a more crushing reform? What if parties were functionally banned from the legislature and from elections altogether? Could partisan actors even recover from that, or would they essentially give up trying to influence government, leaving politicians to behave at their own discretion?

Luckily for party researchers, two states provide convenient test cases for this question. Nebraska has had an officially nonpartisan state legislature since the 1930s. Minnesota had one between 1913 and 1973. I address Minnesota's experiences in the next chapter. Here, I focus on Nebraska, a state famous for its legislature, which is unique both for its nonpartisan rules and its unicameral design.[1]

Less known about the state's legislature is a more recent phenomenon: it is polarizing rapidly—more rapidly than any other state or federal legislative chamber in the nation. A claim of rapid party polarization raises

---

1. This chapter was written in conjunction with Boris M. Shor, Georgetown University.

few eyebrows in modern American politics, of course, as such findings have become commonplace in studies of the Congress and state legislatures. Such a claim warrants particular scrutiny, however, in Nebraska, officially the only nonpartisan state legislature in the land. How does partisanship emerge in a legislature where parties do not officially exist? And how do parties adapt to a reform that essentially bans them from politics?

In this chapter, I examine the recent political history of the Nebraska state legislature through a series of interviews and analyses of campaign donations. I find that the imposition of term limits in the middle of the last decade helped to instigate greater partisan polarization within the chamber. With at least a quarter of the chamber now regularly being turned out of office, a handful of partisan actors, including a Republican governor and many Democratic political operatives, took advantage of situation and became intensely involved with recruiting partisan candidates to run for office and keeping them faithful to a partisan agenda once in office. I compare campaign donation patterns in Nebraska to those of other states with similar financial rules and find Nebraska to have experienced a relatively sharp rise in donor partisanship during this time period. The evidence suggests that Nebraska's legislative political system—once disorganized and unstructured—has developed a more rigid structure in recent years, and this structure is evident both within the chamber and in the elections that send people there. The findings offer a strong demonstration of party adaptation, albeit one that took a great deal of time. Creative policy demanders can impose a partisan government whether the law officially sanctions it or not.

A HISTORY OF NONPARTISANSHIP

Nebraska's voters established their nonpartisan legislature via a statewide initiative in the midst of the Great Depression. US Senator George Norris (R-NE) and others had made the case that the state's bicameral, partisan legislature was needlessly expensive and incompetent—unsuited for dealing with the state's economic difficulties at the time. Despite the opposition of state party leaders, over 90 percent of Nebraska's counties and precincts gave the initiative majority support in 1934 (Sittig 1986). The use of direct democracy in Nebraska's case made it impossible for legislators to reinstate partisanship without the voters' approval. The parties remained virtually nonexistent for decades (Rodgers, Sittig, and Welch 1984; Welch and Carlson 1973; Wright and Schaffner 2002). Welch and Carlson (1973) have found that the establishment of nonpartisanship in 1937 led to a decline in legislative partisanship that never seemed to rebound. Wright and Schaffner's (2002) relatively recent study compared Nebraska with neighboring Kansas, finding the latter to possess a nearly identical demographic and ideological profile to Nebraska's but a substantially more polarized legislature thanks to its partisan elections.

Under state laws, the nonpartisan system affects every aspect of legislative business. There is no official majority or minority caucus in the legislature (known popularly as the Unicam), nor are there whips or party leaders. The speaker is elected by his colleagues through a secret ballot, as are the chairs of all the standing committees. The 49 senators are elected to staggered four-year terms via nonpartisan ballot. The primary election is an open, blanket contest, with all eligible candidates for a legislative seat appearing on every ballot regardless of the voters' or candidates' party registrations. The ballots are constitutionally forbidden from containing information about the state legislative candidates' affiliations with political parties. The top two winners of the primary go onto a similarly nonpartisan November runoff election, even if they are registered with the same political party.

Just because the ballots lack evidence of party affiliation does not mean that it is impossible to determine the partisan leanings of legislative candidates in Nebraska. Newspaper and online coverage of campaigns often refers explicitly to the party affiliations of the candidates, and researchers and political activists can readily learn this information from the media, from state legislative voter records, and from a roster published by the state government. Still, the typical voter is less likely to pay such information collection costs when making a choice between state legislative candidates, and it seems reasonable to say that most voters, who see party labels on neither the primary nor the general election ballot, have little idea which candidates belong to which parties. Such institutional rules certainly do not favor partisan behavior among legislators.

However, recent roll call evidence suggests that the Unicam is polarizing. In their innovative study of state legislative roll call votes over the past two decades, Shor and McCarty (2013) place state legislator ideal points in a common space so that we can compare them across states and years. That is, they calculate ideal points—numerical estimates of the ideological left-right positions of legislators—based on roll call votes, and these scores can be compared across chambers and over time. They find that despite Nebraska's nonpartisan charter, its chamber doesn't stand out as unusually depolarized. Quite the opposite, actually: according to Shor and McCarty's measures, Nebraska's Unicam has polarized more quickly over the past decade than any of the other 98 state legislative chambers or even the US House and Senate.

Figure 4.1 charts patterns in legislative polarization for every state legislative chamber since 1993. The Nebraska Unicam is highlighted in the figure. As can be seen, Nebraska actually saw the lowest level of polarization in the nation back in the mid-1990s, but it has quickly surpassed many other states, with a dramatic increase in polarization coming in the second half of the last decade. In 2010, it was about as polarized as Kansas, the state against which it fared so poorly in terms of legislative partisanship just a decade earlier (Wright and Schaffner 2002).

How is this possible? Party leaders and activists have made no secret of their desire to reinstate partisanship, but roughly a score of formal attempts to do so over the past 75 years have failed to secure sufficient votes from legislators or signatures from voters (Sittig 1986). Even if party activists want to see more ideologically extreme candidates winning their party's nomination, it is no small thing to get those candidates past voters in a nonpartisan blanket primary election. Primary voters, after all, must choose among a handful of candidates, often of multiple parties, without

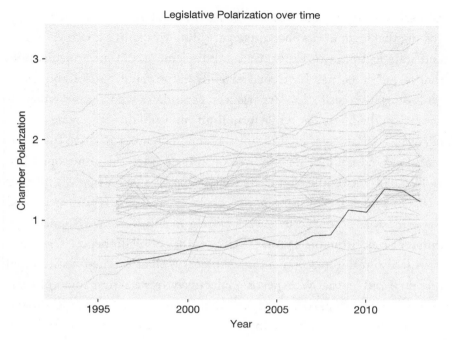

Figure 4.1 Polarization of 99 State Legislatures over Time.
NOTE: Chamber polarization is measured as the difference between the median party
ideal points within each state legislative chamber. Nebraska's Unicam is highlighted.
Data come from Shor/McCarty (2014). Chart generated by Boris Shor.

the aid of party labels. What would allow them to coordinate on the most
ideologically extreme—but still electable—candidate?

One possible explanation is the rise of term limits in Nebraska.
Nebraskans actually passed term limits in 1992, but that initiative was
invalidated by the state's Supreme Court. After several other attempts, an
initiative limiting state legislators to two consecutive four-year terms was
passed by the voters in 2000 and started turning out incumbents in 2006.
We would expect to find the most profound impact of term limits on state
politics occurring in 2006, at the moment it began affecting the composition
of the legislature (and this is consistent with the trend seen in Figure 4.1),
but given that its enactment seemed nearly inevitable since the early 1990s,
we might expect to see political actors adapting to it prior to ratification.

Term limits have been associated with heightened partisanship in state
legislatures (Bailey and Sinclair 2009), although other studies have found

no such link (Cain and Kousser 2004). Beer (2001) finds evidence suggesting that term limits encourage party-line voting in Mexico's national and state legislatures. Kurtz, Cain, and Niemi (2007), meanwhile, note that term limits may have inadvertently empowered parties and interest groups by creating less experienced candidates who are more dependent upon them. That is, while term limits may not directly create a more partisan legislature, they do unmistakably increase legislative turnover; seats held by incumbents for three or four decades will come open just as frequently as battleground districts. This creates an opportunity for partisan actors to play a more direct role in candidate recruitment, and the legislators produced by such a system may behave in systematically different ways from ones protected by decades of incumbency. Term limits will also result in a pool of officeholders with attenuated institutional memory and legislative expertise, effectively transferring some of their political power to parties, lobbyists, and the executive branch (Cain and Kousser 2004). Finally, term limits introduce a large number of freshmen with no commitments to longstanding chamber norms, such as bipartisanship. Such an influx of new members can cause these norms to collapse (Diermeier 1995).

Have term limits had such an impact on Nebraska politics? To address this topic, I have conducted a series of interviews with political actors across the ideological spectrum in Nebraska politics. These actors include officeholders, party officials, journalists, interest groups leaders, and prominent donors. In the next section, I provide some of the evidence offered by these qualitative data. The section that follows seeks to match the interview responses up with a quantitative examination of sources of polarization in Nebraska.

(NON) PARTISANSHIP IN NEBRASKA: AN ASSESSMENT FROM THE INSIDE

In meeting with incumbents in the Nebraska Unicam, one of the most consistently expressed opinions is a clear and nearly unanimous love for the nonpartisan system.[2] "We really are a family in this legislature," boasts Senator Amanda McGill,[3] a registered Democrat[4] from Lincoln. "I am just as good of friends with the Republicans in the body as I am the Democrats." Unicam speaker Mike Flood,[5] a registered Republican from Norfolk, echoes, "If you come down to Lincoln and expect to see people vote with what you think the core principles of the party are every time, you're going to be sorely disappointed." One such disappointed observer is David Kramer, the former chairman of the Nebraska Republican Party. According to Kramer, "There are people who've been elected to the body who I've known to be great partisans, who have gone to great lengths since they've been elected to the body to try and be less partisan than they were when they went in the body."

Speaker Flood adds that the nonpartisan system creates a somewhat chaotic environment in which there are no standing coalitions: "There's no caucusing. . . . There's no minority, majority whip. Every issue requires the hustle of every vote." Instead, relatively consistent coalitions form around particular issues, including abortion and urban or rural issues, but those coalitions regularly transcend party lines.

Despite this celebration of the nonpartisan tradition, there is an acknowledgment that the chamber has become somewhat more partisan in recent years. "There are still some moderates," says United Transportation Union lobbyist Ray Lineweber,[6] "but not as many as years past." One might look to the state parties themselves as the cause of this— party leaders have sought for years to strengthen their role relative to the legislature and even to formally reintroduce partisanship, only to be

2. Interviews in this section took place in 2011. Many of the interview subjects are officeholders who no longer hold the positions they held at the time of the interview. I refer to subjects by the titles they held at the time of the interview, although I note in the endnotes how those titles have changed.

3. McGill was termed out of the Unicam in 2015.

4. While members of the Nebraska Unicam run on nonpartisan ballots, and their offices and legislative journals bear no indication of their party allegiances, I have nonetheless included senators' party registrations—information that the subjects themselves volunteered—in this section.

5. Flood was termed out of the Unicam in 2013.

6. Lineweber retired from the union in 2012.

rebuffed by legislators content with the nonpartisan system. According to Senator McGill, "I sometimes feel like the Democratic Party, particularly in Nebraska, puts a little too much emphasis on what's in the platform. . . . I don't feel they should really be pushing issues on the elected officials here." According to former state Republican chair David Kramer,

> The legislature was not particularly receptive to having the party involved in much, once the elections got over. You know, they all wanted our help at election time. . . . They did not often appreciate that the party took positions on key legislative issues, did not appreciate that we would communicate publicly with them what our positions were on those issues, and encourage them to vote one way or another. . . . We were trying to partisanize the legislature, and that was unbecoming of the body, and you know, I'm not sure when or where being partisan became a bad word.

Nebraska's term-limits initiative, which began terming out members in 2006, had a dramatic effect on the chamber's composition. The percentage of freshmen in the Unicam, usually hovering between 15 and 20 percent (Niemi and Powell 2004), shot up to nearly 50 percent after the 2006 elections. When the 101st legislature was sworn in on January 7, 2009, only 12 of the chamber's 49 senators had been in the chamber four years earlier. Term limits had removed many longstanding incumbents, requiring someone to recruit new candidates to run. That job largely fell to Nebraska's formal parties.

Barry Rubin, who had just moved from Maryland to become the chairman of Nebraska's Democratic Party in 2004, saw term limits as a unique opportunity for aggressive recruitment. "From a tactical standpoint," Rubin says, "[term limits were] great for the Democratic Party, because it opened up seats where . . . we haven't been able to compete more for in years." Rubin and others then went about finding candidates: "We would literally scour the earth looking for good, moderate, forward-thinking candidates that we could find to run for office." One such candidate was Amanda McGill, who in 2006 had been a communications director for the state Democratic Party: "Before I knew it, my own colleagues had recruited me to run for the state legislature. So, it wasn't something I was planning on doing." According to Rubin, such recruitment could get very detailed if a solid candidate was not initially obvious:

> I've literally spent days and days along with some of my coworkers going through registered voter files data and scouring the data for "five of five" Democrats—"five of five" meaning they've voted in five of the last five elections—who, in looking at occupational codes and looking at income and things of that nature and figuring out, "Okay, here's a lawyer who votes in every election," and we'll sit around with a group of five or ten people from different walks of life that are all like-minded organizations or party people or whatever and said, "Yeah, I know that guy. He's a lawyer down the street; he's real active in politics. . . ." That was how we would target them and pick up the phone and say, "Hey, you ever thought about running for office?"

Recruitment efforts didn't end at just identifying good candidates. Both parties, according to Kramer, "work like crazy in these nonpartisan races to support candidates of their particular persuasion. . . . We probably targeted four to six legislative races a cycle, and put thousands of dollars into those races." Rubin says that the Democratic Party wouldn't just hand money to candidates, but would still help them raise their own funds: "We provided them with leads. . . . We had a finance staff that helped them do call sheets and call time with them and things of that nature or hire their own people to set up those operations." With fundraising in place, Rubin says, the party would also train their candidates in best campaign practices at a campaigning "school":

> We did a campaign camp in '05 and a campaign camp before this '06 cycle; we did two campaign camps, and we took . . . anybody who was interested in running for office, anybody who was interested in working for a candidate, brought them in, brought in some of the

best people in the business. We had top-of-the-line pollsters; we had top-of-the-line media consultants, national DC high-level meeting consultants, telemarketing vendors, direct mail vendors, the whole nine yards. Brought some of the best in the business.

To the extent they could, the party leaders coordinated their recruiting efforts with allied interest groups. According to former GOP chair Kramer, "We would collaborate with other organizations that, you know, shared similar kinds of interests. The Chamber [of Commerce] being one of them, the National Federation of Independent Business, the realtors, other organizations that, while not overtly political themselves, their philosophy of governance generally meshed closer to ours than it did to others." Former Democratic chair Rubin echoes this:

Sitting around the table with us on many occasions were some lobbyists, were special interest groups, labor organizations, environmental organizations, civil rights or human rights organizations. . . . So you'd have the AFL-CIO or the NEA or the Sierra Club or whomever. Some business groups, too. We had to use our collective resources and intelligence to figure out where we were going to find folks and then coordinate together how we were going use our limited resources as one and get these folks elected.

Terry Moore, the president of the Omaha Federation of Labor, boasts, "There's a multitude [of legislators] that are in there right now that we recruited—probably about four or five of them that I personally recruited and brought in front of our board through our system." Other interest group leaders claimed an active role in candidate recruitment, as well. Julie Schmit-Albin of Nebraska Right to Life, for examples, says, "We network with certain like-minded people who are also looking for good candidates, as long as they understand that anyone they send our way has to pass our pro-life endorsement criteria."

The marriage of parties and interest groups on the task of candidate recruitment served several valuable functions. First, it helped ensure that whichever candidates were preferred would have a strong advantage over any late-arriving candidate whose ideological dispositions might be inconsistent with the party's. Second, it helped avoid difficult primary fights with allies. As Rubin sums up, "Come up with one person that we can all agree on and jump in the pool together, 'cause otherwise we're just going to kill each other."

Another actor who has been extremely active in recruiting candidates is Nebraska's Republican governor, Dave Heineman.[7] Heineman ascended to the governor's office in 2005—at roughly the same time that term limits kicked in and that Rubin began running the Democratic Party's efforts. Heineman's experience within his party is somewhat atypical for Nebraska governors: a former executive director of the state's Republican Party, Heineman is seen as an exceptionally partisan creature with a hands-on approach to politicking. According to Senator Heath Mello, a registered Democrat from Omaha, "We've seen a level of involvement from the executive branch that we haven't seen before, in regards to recruiting candidates ... hand-picking candidates, raising funds and expending funds on legislative candidates' behalf." Senator McGill found herself going toe to toe with the governor in her 2010 reelection campaign:

> The governor was the one who appeared on the mail pieces against me ... supporting my opponent. So, I may trust most of my Republican colleagues in the legislature, but I have no love for the governor in particular, because I know he was trying to get me unelected.

Having so many members of the Unicam personally indebted to him has given the governor considerable power over the legislative branch. Beyond that, term limits have created a larger contingent of junior legislators with little experience or institutional knowledge who are more dependent upon the governor's office for information and resources. "Our governor is very active in the processes here," says Senator Beau McCoy, a registered Republican from Omaha. "His office is obviously in the building

---

7. Heineman was termed out of office in 2015.

here in our Capitol. He makes the rounds. . . . He'll poke his head in our office from time to time just to say hi." Lobbyist Walt Radcliffe adds, "We . . . seem to have more of a unicameral parliament than anything else. The governor would have to really come up with something pretty wacky to not get what he wants."

In general, the new party involvement in elections is seen as a cause of increased party influence over the legislature. Rubin summarizes, "There's a lot more unity and a lot more collaboration on the Republican side in the Unicameral based on the fact that this Republican state party has a big role, or had a big role, in getting a lot of those folks elected." Increased interest group activity in elections, combined with declining institutional knowledge, has also helped interest group lobbyists gain power in the chamber. According to Jennifer Carter of the group Nebraska Appleseed, "We actually have a little bit more of an influence there and credibility than we used to, so in that sense, it can be easier for us to work with senators, have them listen to us, transfer information, that kind of stuff."

THE MOST IMPORTANT ACTORS

To get a more representative sense of the structure of Nebraska politics, I asked respondents who they believed would be the three most important people to contact if one were interested in running for the state legislature. The answers suggest that formal party sources are overwhelmingly seen as essential for those interested in mounting a campaign for office. Among Democrats, party officials, including the chairman and the executive director, were the dominant recommended actors, along with current or former state senators from the area. This was generally suggested for the purpose of giving the prospective candidate a sense of what the job would be like, although several respondents suggested this as a specific source of recruitment. A middle tier of actors includes the mayor of Lincoln, the staff of US Senator Ben Nelson, and prominent donors. A few lobbying organizations and consultants rounded out the bottom of the list. Even if pooled together, the interest groups do not nearly rise to the level of the party sources in citations.

On the Republican side, the lesson was roughly the same. Judging from the interviews, respondents of both parties broadly saw the governor as the de facto head of the state Republican Party and its chief strategist. Thus it is not surprising to find that Governor Heineman was the number-one choice among Republicans as a crucial actor in legislative campaigns. As on the Democratic side, respondents advised speaking to incumbent senators, party staff, and the staff of Speaker Mike Flood. Donors received somewhat higher billing here than on the Democratic side.

One shouldn't overinterpret these results as the survey sample was neither particularly large nor randomly selected. However, they do offer some insight into the mindset of Nebraska's political elites, who clearly believe that the formal parties and the governor are pivotal actors in legislative campaigns. These results suggest a good deal of formal, but often barely visible, structure to Nebraska's current political system. They also suggest that while interest groups and donors may be important, they are subservient to the formal parties and the governor in the matter of recruitment.

AN EMPIRICAL TEST OF STRUCTURE

The interviews made clear that this structure did not always exist. Term limits, it was noted, gave the parties the incentive and the opportunity to organize state politics in a way impossible previously. As Senator Mello remarked, "Term limits [have] ushered in, I think, a level of partisanship that most people would agree that they haven't seen before." Has their increased role in recruitment given the parties the influence over legislators they have long sought?

It is certainly possible that some of the reported change in the attitudes and beliefs of Nebraska's political class is post hoc rationalization. However, we might expect to see the behavior of political actors change in observable ways with the advent of term limits. We know from the common space roll call data in Shor and McCarty (2013) that legislative polarization was increasing at an extremely high rate in the state throughout this time. The session at which we would expect polarization to increase the most as a result of term limits would be 2007–8, which is exactly when the measured ideological distance between the parties sees its most rapid rise. In 2006 the distance was around 0.72, while in 2008 it was 0.84 and 2010 at was 1.1. It continued rising to 1.4 in 2011–12, although dropped a bit to 1.25 in 2013. By comparison, in 1996, the level was 0.467.

Another expected change in elite behavior would be a shift in the patterns of campaign donations. If a partisan structure emerged in the middle of the decade as a result of term limits, then we would expect a reflection in donation patterns. In a relatively weak party system, we would not expect to see elite donors giving exclusively to one party. Rather, they would donate for any number of idiosyncratic reasons—ideology, friendships, reputation, and so on. Conversely, if parties are strong, it makes sense to donate exclusively to one party.

The donation patterns of the Nebraska Republican and Democratic parties (NRP and NDP, respectively) reflect this expectation to some extent. In the three election cycles prior to the imposition of term limits in 2006, the NRP donated $20,657 to candidates, but $27,304 in the three subsequent elections. The shift was even starker for Democrats; the NDP donated $6,551 in the three cycles prior to term limits and $36,906 in the three cycles thereafter. But these are fairly paltry sums, donated to only a handful of legislative candidates. Party activity, to the extent it occurred, would likely be best captured by the activities of a broader range of donors loosely affiliated with, but loyal to, the party (Hassell 2013).

We wouldn't necessarily expect to detect much of a shifting contribution pattern among all donors—low-level donors are known to be inconsistent in their preferences and attached to just one or two candidates. But elite donors—those who make large donations and set donation patterns followed by others—should indicate such a tendency (Graf and Reeher 2006).

To examine the behavior of elite donors in Nebraska, I have collected campaign finance records for state legislative races from 2000 to 2010 from the National Institute on Money in State Politics.[8] For my first analysis, I have set a lower limit of $2000 in year 2000 dollars[9] for all state legislative contributions by a donor. This eliminates most of the donors from analysis. In 2000, for example, a total of 674 unique donors made 2463 contributions to state legislative campaigns in Nebraska. There were only 45 donors that year giving at least $2000 to state legislative candidates, however, making 106 such contributions. Reducing the number of cases this way allows us to make the pattern clearer graphically without including excessive data that don't actually affect the underlying results.

A quick comparison between two different years within the dataset offers some stark contrasts. Elite donors in 2000 often contributed to candidates across party lines. The Nebraska State Education Association, for example, distributed $8500 across three legislative candidates who were registered Republicans, while giving another $21,732 to five Democratic candidates. The Nebraska Realtors' Association, meanwhile, donated $9000 to four Republican candidates and $5000 to two Democrats. Indeed, most of the major donors that year were quite bipartisan in their contribution patterns. This is a stark contrast from 2008, in which major donors tended to stick within their party.

To get a better sense of the changes in partisan funding patterns, I borrow some graphing techniques from social network analysis. Figure 4.2 shows a network graph of Nebraska state legislators in 2000. Each dot, or "node," represents a candidate. They are connected by lines, or "edges," if they share a common donor. That is, if George Soros donates $2000 to Candidate A and $2000 to Candidate B, A and B will have a line connecting them in the graph, representing the donor they have in common. In the figure, squares represent registered Democrats, circles indicate registered Republicans, and triangles demark independent candidates.

As the figure shows, nearly every Republican candidate is connected to a Democrat, and nearly every Democratic candidate is connected to a Republican, via elite donors. The donor space is depolarized. In other

8. http://www.followthemoney.org.
9. I have used the consumer price index to measure inflation. $2000 in the year 2000 is the equivalent of $2533 in the year 2010.

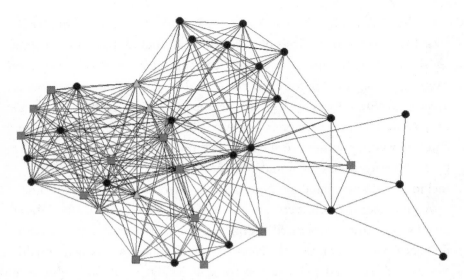

Figure 4.2 Network of Candidates for Nebraska Unicam, 2000.
NOTES: Each node represents a candidate for the Nebraska legislature in 2000. Red circles depict registered Republicans, blue squares are registered Democrats, and independents are marked by green triangles. The candidates are connected if they share an elite donor (one who has contributed at least $2,000).

words, if a major donor contributed $2000 to a Democrat, she almost certainly contributed that much to a Republican, as well. While Democrats are somewhat clustered to the left of the diagram, it is difficult to identify a faction of either Republicans or Democrats in the network.

Compare that network to the one from 2008, depicted in Figure 4.3. Here, we see that the network of candidates connected by donors has changed dramatically from a few years earlier. Instead of one large community of candidates, we see two distinct factions, divided largely along party lines.

Figures 4.2 and 4.3 suggest that some change occurred over the last decade. Several examinations of these network structures suggest that donation patterns have simply become more partisan; elite donors simply aren't spreading money across party lines the way they used to. To the extent that candidates and officeholders in Nebraska are obligated to their donors, those donors are compelling them to behave in an increasingly partisan fashion.

We can further examine the rising role of partisanship in Nebraska campaign donations by looking at contribution patterns. It may be, that is, that the

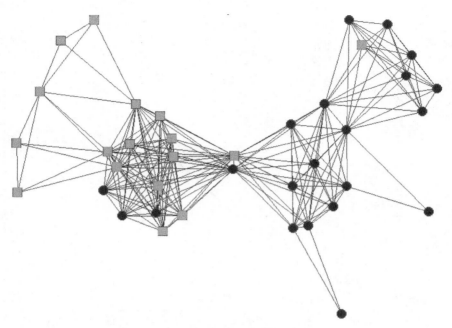

Figure 4.3 Network of Candidates for Nebraska Unicam, 2008.
NOTES: Analysis is limited to those who contributed at least $500 (in year 2000 dollars) in state legislative races to more than one candidate in more than one year. "Dem-leaning" donors are those who gave at least 80% of their donations to Democratic legislative candidates; "GOPleaning" are those who gave at least 80% of their donations to Republican candidates. The remaining donors are categorized as "bipartisan."

people who make major donations to Nebraska state legislative races today are more politically polarized than the donors who contributed a few years ago. A simple analysis along these lines can be seen in Figure 4.4, which shows the partisan contribution patterns of repeat donors, focusing on those who gave at least $500 (in year 2000 dollars) to at least two state legislative candidates in at least two years. I have categorized the donors based on their donation patterns. If they made at least 80 percent of their donations to Democratic state legislative candidates, I have categorized them as "Dem-leaning." Conversely, those labeled "GOP-leaning" contributed at least 80 percent of their donations to Republican legislative candidates. The rest are categorized as "bipartisan." The figure charts the percentage of each donor group in each year.

As can be seen, Dem-leaning donors have generally comprised a low percentage of contributors, but that number increased slowly during the

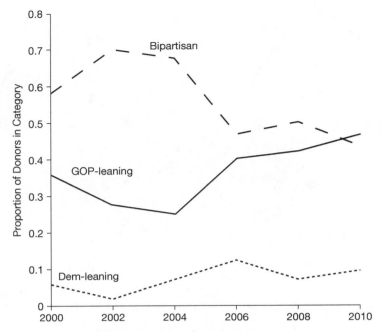

Figure 4.4 Trends among Repeat Donors.
NOTES: Analysis is limited to those who contributed at least $500 (in year 2000 dollars) in state legislative races to more than one candidate in more than one year. "Dem-leaning" donors are those who gave at least 80% of their donations to Democratic legislative candidates; "GOP-leaning" are those who gave at least 80% of their donations to Republican candidates. The remaining donors are categorized as "bipartisan."

decade and jumped substantially between 2004 and 2006. The percentage of donors categorized as GOP-leaning also took a sharp upward turn after 2004. For both groups of party-leaning donors, their proportion of the donor pool each year under term limits has been higher than it was in any year prior to term limits. Bipartisan donors, meanwhile, have been on the decline, most sharply after 2004. This suggests that donors in Nebraska legislative elections are polarizing. State legislators are being funded by an increasingly partisan group of elite donors.

Another take on changing fundraising patterns can be seen in Figure 4.5. Here, I have divided up Nebraska's legislators by their ideal points (as calculated by Shor and McCarty 2013). Those whose ideal point's absolute value is greater than the absolute value of their party's median ideal

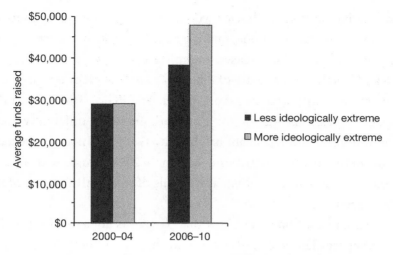

Figure 4.5 Campaign Fundraising Patterns by Ideological Extremism.
NOTE: The plot shows the fundraising records of Nebraska legislators, divided into two camps by their ideological extremism, proxied by whether the absolute value of their legislative ideal point was greater than the absolute value of their party's median ("more ideologically extreme") or less than the absolute value of their party's median ("less ideologically extreme").

point are classified as more ideologically extreme; the rest are considered less ideologically extreme. As the figure shows, there was little difference in the fundraising prowess of legislators across the ideological spectrum in the early part of the decade. Regardless of ideological extremism, legislative candidates prior to term limits raised an average of $29,000. Under term limits, however, we have seen a substantial divergence between these candidates. While candidates across the board are raising more money than they used to, the more ideologically extreme legislative candidates are each raising approximately $10,000 more than their moderate counterparts. This is suggestive of a recent change in fundraising patterns, and it is consistent with other evidence suggesting that the electoral environment has become more favorable to a more polarized set of candidates.

I perform a more sophisticated analysis on these donation patterns to include appropriate statistical controls. Studying campaign contribution patterns, however, can present some challenges. One large problem is the possibility that donors influence each other. That is, one donation to a candidate may encourage friends or colleagues of the donor to make a

similar donation. Such behavior would mean that the act of contributing is not an independent one, making analyses of such patterns produce
results that are potentially biased and misleading.

To address this, I make use of a network analysis technique called the
exponential-family random graph model, or ERGM. This is essentially
a logistic regression equation for a network, in which different variables
are used to predict the probability that any two given nodes have a connection between them (Park and Newman 2004; Snijders et al. 2006;
Wasserman and Pattison 1996). The details of this analysis can be found
in the Appendix.

The basic results, however, show that party was not a reliable predictor
of whether legislators shared a common donor in 2000–2004, prior to
term limits. Under term limits (2006–10), however, party does become
a statistically significant predictor. We can get a sense of this change by
examining Figure 4.6, which converts the ERGM results into predicted
probabilities (see Appendix for details). This figure charts the probability of any two given candidates sharing a common donor based on the
similarity of their ideal points and whether or not they share a political party. In 2000 (at left), we can see a modest effect for ideology—the
more ideologically distant the candidates, the less likely they are to have
a donor in common. Party, on the other hand, seems not to matter at all.

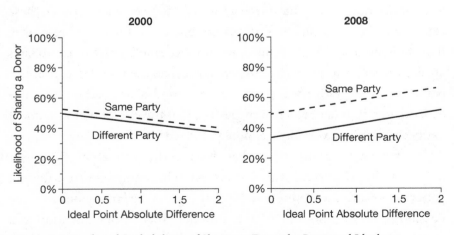

Figure 4.6 Predicted Probabilities of Sharing a Donor by Party and Ideology.

Copartisans are only 3 percent more likely to share a donor than cross-partisans, a result that is not statistically significant.

The chart at right shows the probabilities for 2008, during the term-limits era. While the figure appears to indicate that candidates are more likely to share a donor the more ideologically distant they are from each other, that coefficient is actually statistically insignificant. Party, however, suddenly matters a great deal; copartisans are 15 percent more likely to share a donor than cross-partisans. These results suggest that party has become more important to structuring elite donations since the advent of term limits.

We can increase our confidence in these findings by exploring counterfactuals suggested by other states. That is, while I have made efforts to control for confounding factors, it is possible that Nebraska simply experienced a regional or national polarizing trend in campaign donation patterns that have happened beyond the state's borders as well. To examine this possibility, I collected identical state legislative campaign contributions records from nine other control states over the same time period. These nine states—Alabama, Iowa, Indiana, Missouri, North Dakota, Oregon, Pennsylvania, Texas, and Utah—were selected because they, like Nebraska, have no upper limit on contributions to state legislative candidates. And while partisanship may have increased in those states, none of the states adopted term limits during this time period. I gathered campaign finance records from these states from the National Institute on Money in State Politics.[10]

To compare the states, I look at all donor ties between state legislative candidates between 2000 and 2010 and measure the percentage of those ties occurring between legislators of the same party. I estimate this once for 2000–2004 (prior to term limits in Nebraska) and once for 2006–10 (after the adoption of term limits in Nebraska). I expect, due to polarizing trends, that all the states will see increases in the percentage of donor ties occurring within the same party. However, if the increase is atypically

---

10. Mississippi and Virginia also fit this description. However, there was insufficient available public campaign finance data to include them in the analysis.

Table 4.1 DONOR POLARIZATION IN TEN
STATES WITH NO UPPER CONTRIBUTION LIMIT
FOR LEGISLATIVE RACES

State	2000–2004	2006–10	Increase
Utah	48.12	72.80	24.69
Pennsylvania	48.81	57.52	8.71
Nebraska	38.37	44.54	6.17
Texas	49.56	53.73	4.17
Oregon	59.06	62.50	3.44
Alabama	52.88	54.47	1.59
Indiana	60.18	61.12	0.94
Missouri	55.94	55.41	−0.53
Iowa	65.38	58.19	−7.18
North Dakota	95.79	88.36	−7.43
Mean	57.41	60.86	3.46
Median	54.41	57.86	2.51

NOTE: Donor polarization is measured as the percent
of candidate network ties, via shared donors, that are
between candidates of the same party.

large in Nebraska relative to the other states, that would suggest that
Nebraska's rise in polarization is attributable to specific events within
that state rather than from larger national trends.

The results of the analysis, which are displayed in Table 4.1, suggest that
Nebraska has a generally low rate of donor polarization relative to the other
states, but saw a substantial rise in donor polarization under term limits.
The greatest rate of polarization was observed in Utah, with an astound-
ing 25 point increase between the two time periods.[11] Pennsylvania comes
in second with an 8.7 point increase, followed closely by Nebraska at 6.2
points. This is well above the median (2.5) or mean (3.5) increases between
the two eras. Although the small number of cases prevents this difference
from meeting conventional tests of statistical significance, it does suggest
that Nebraska has experienced a greater-than-average polarization of its

11. This is likely a product of a conservative insurgency and resulting intraparty skirmishes
within the Utah Republican Party at the end of the last decade, largely focused on nomination procedures (Quin Monson, email interview, September 24, 2015).

elite donors base, that it has come to more closely resemble other states (those with parties) in the way it funds state legislative races, and that this shift was roughly concurrent with the adoption of term limits.

DISCUSSION

Assessing a state's partisanship is no simple task. Just as there are multiple facets of parties (legislative caucuses, voter allegiances, formal and informal organizations, etc.), so are there multiple ways of describing just how important parties are in a given state and how that role may have changed over time.

Nonetheless, using a variety of methods, I have sought to do just this for the state of Nebraska. The results suggest that while early 20th-century reformers were largely successful at reducing the impact of parties on the state government, partisanship has returned to Nebraska with a vengeance in the past few years. To be sure, the Nebraska Unicam is hardly the California Assembly, no less the British House of Commons; there is considerable ideological overlap between the parties and legislators deeply value their nonpartisan tradition. Voting coalitions, several senators suggested, do not regularly follow party divisions, but rather fall along splits determined by particular issues stances, and bill authors must sometimes build winning coalitions from the ground up.

And yet the preponderance of evidence suggests that this familiar system is giving way to a more partisan one. The forced retirement of a large segment of the legislature in 2006 due to term limits spurred the parties and the governor into action, recruiting, training, and funding candidates at levels not previously seen in modern Nebraska. The state's new legislators are increasingly being chosen for their expected adherence to party agendas, as determined by party leaders and the governor. And the donation patterns of elite campaign contributors are increasingly following a partisan and ideological pattern, suggesting that to the extent that legislators want to keep their donors happy, they will do so by voting more with their party.

This is not to suggest that the trends I report here from 2000 to 2010 will continue unabated. Indeed, roll call voting records from 2013 suggest that polarization in the Nebraska legislature has plateaued recently (Figure 4.1). The trends of donor polarization and ideological candidate recruitment do not appear to have reversed. However, we did see evidence of a bipartisan pushback against the termed-out governor Heineman as his tenure drew to a close in 2014. In a follow-up interview in June of 2014, Senator Heath Mello remarked, "I think over the last few years, we've seen a move towards a more independent voting pattern away from what the governor has been advocating in the legislature." Indeed, as Mello noted, majorities in the chamber, including large numbers of Republicans, have overridden several of the governor's recent vetoes on education issues, road construction bonds, and health-care funding (Schulte 2014). This may well represent the flip side of term limits—even as it may open the door to greater partisanship in recruitment, those compelling partisan behavior lose much of their power as they become termed out themselves.

Nonetheless, Nebraska's political system experienced a significant shock in the middle of the last decade and appears unlikely to return to its earlier nonpartisan style. As the parties continue to recruit candidates in an ideological fashion and as the influence of colleagues from an earlier, less partisan era fades away, we are likely to see increased legislative polarization there in the coming years. It took decades, but the reform designed to drive partisanship from the legislature has essentially been undone.

Why, then, did Nebraska's version of antiparty reform—the nonpartisan legislature—apparently work for so long, while parties in other states seem to adapt and overcome antiparty reforms relatively quickly, as in the Colorado example from the previous chapter? A good parallel for Nebraska's story is that of California under cross-filing (1913–59), under which candidates could run in as many primaries as they desired without their party label appearing on the ballot, which substantially depressed legislative partisanship for four decades. Other states have attempted to limit partisanship and empower moderate candidates through the creation of more open primary elections, with little apparent success (McGhee et al. 2014).

Why might parties be able to adapt to some of these reforms but not to a ballot without party labels? The latter has the feature of depriving voters of one of the most essential pieces of information the ballot has to offer—arguably, more important than the identity of the candidates themselves. Yes, highly informed voters, political activists, and others can likely discern the real Democrats and Republicans on the ballots, but the vast majority of voters will not conduct research on these matters prior to entering the polling booth and are at the mercy of whatever information actually appears on the ballot. The fact that party labels still do not appear next to the names of Nebraska's Unicam candidates will certainly continue to provide a ceiling on legislative partisanship there, since many voters still lack the necessary information to vote their party. Nonetheless, it appears that the parties themselves are developing ways to structure elections in a more partisan manner and give advantages to their preferred candidates.

In California, what brought about the end of cross-filing was direct democracy—ironically the very thing that introduced it originally. Voters passed an initiative putting party labels back on the ballot in 1952, and partisan voting patterns and legislative organization resumed very quickly. In Nebraska, it appears that another initiative—term limits—is effecting a similar change, providing an opportunity for the party to reassert itself.

5

The Nonpartisan Legislature
in Minnesota

The account of Nebraska in the previous chapter is an instructive one. Even though the ballot there remains nonpartisan, party elites, including high-level donors and elected party leaders, have helped to polarize the legislature in recent years. Thus even in one of the most challenging environments for parties—a chamber of legislators elected via nonpartisan ballot—entrepreneurial party leaders are able to overcome institutional rules and compel some partisan behavior from their elected officials.

But perhaps Nebraska is a fluke. After all, is the experience of one state over the span of just a few years really representative of the sort of thing that could happen all over the country? Fortunately, we have a similar case available for examination, that of Minnesota. That state adopted nonpartisanship for its legislature in 1913, but then switched back to partisan elections 60 years later. Did the reintroduction of party balloting bring about the expected sharp increase in legislative partisanship?

Actually, this shift coincided with only a very small (and debatable) increase in intraparty cohesion, and it did not seem to affect the ideological distance between the parties. The reason, I suggest, that the adoption of partisan elections had such a minimal effect on legislators is that legislators themselves had already adopted ideological coalitions within the chamber (Liberals and Conservatives), coalitions that were enforced by interest groups outside the chamber. The adoption of partisan elections thus corrected a fiction but did little to affect life inside the chamber. The results are instructive about the nature of legislative parties. While the electoral connection (Mayhew 1974) is certainly useful, it is not absolutely necessary for legislative partisanship. That can be created and enforced by legislators and policy demanders without input from the voters.

The chapter begins by looking at some previous findings on legislative parties and the expected effects of switching from partisan to nonpartisan elections and vice versa. I then proceed to describe Minnesota's unusual experience with partisanship, including its unexpected (and, indeed, accidental) abolition of parties in 1913, the emergence of ideological coalitions within the chamber in the mid-20th century, and the readoption of partisan elections in the 1970s. I analyze legislative behavior from the 1960s through the 1980s with a collection of interest group ratings. I conclude with suggestions for what the findings teach us about the nature of parties.

PARTY LABELS AND PARTISAN EFFECTS

Some two-thirds of America's legislative bodies, including the vast majority of city councils and county commissions, are nonpartisan. The decision to make so many of these bodies nonpartisan dates back to the Progressive Era of the early 20th century. Progressives delineated a belief that the parties were corrupt institutions that improperly intervened between voters and elected officials and that a government free of parties could be run more efficiently and effectively (Rosenblum 2008). It was further argued that, while parties might be appropriate for national government, they had no place in the less ideological decisions of local government. "The time is near," said one Progressive Minnesota journalist in 1914, "when men will be chosen for public positions in state and city, village and county, upon their honesty and fitness instead of how they line up on national issues that have no necessary relation to state and local affairs" (quoted in Adrian 1952b, 163).

Charles Adrian provided some of the pioneering research on nonpartisanship in American elections. Adrian (1952a) delineated several expectations of nonpartisan elections. One was that they would weaken party organizations; party machinery would tend to atrophy, as it would have fewer material rewards to offer people interested in politics. Another was that politicians would tend to segregate into mutually exclusive partisan and nonpartisan career paths. That is, the decision to enter nonpartisan office would tend to preclude a politician from seeking higher partisan office, and vice versa. The overall thrust of Adrian's work suggests important and far-reaching results from a chamber's decision to become nonpartisan, affecting party actors, and current and future candidates well outside its offices.

Later research supports this view. Jenkins (2000) finds that members of the Confederate Congress—which mirrored the institutional structure of the US Congress except for a lack of parties—voted with less ideological constraint than they did when they had previously served in Washington. Schaffner, Streb, and Wright (2001) compare partisan and nonpartisan elections across similar constituencies and find that the shift to nonpartisanship is associated with lower voter turnout and stronger incumbency advantages. Nonpartisan elections also seem to be associated with substantial ballot rolloff, as many voters in partisan contests have little basis on which to evaluate candidates in nonpartisan races (Schaffner and Streb 2002; Squire and Smith 1988). Several studies of Nebraska politics have found that state's nonpartisan legislature to have nearly structureless coalitional voting patterns (Aldrich and Battista 2002; Welch and Carlson 1973; Wright and Schaffner 2002), although some more recent work, including my previous chapter, finds evidence of partisan voting patterns emerging (Masket and Shor 2015; Shor, Berry, and McCarty 2010). In general, determine Wright, Osborn, and Winburn (2004), the lack of stable legislative coalitions in nonpartisan legislatures undermines the connection between voter preferences and legislative policy outcomes.

A few studies have focused specifically on Minnesota's shift to partisanship in the 1970s and its effect on mass voting behavior. Schaffner, Streb, and Wright (2001) find a detectable, but only modest, decline in ballot rolloff in Minnesota senate elections when comparing 1972 (under nonpartisanship) with 1976 (under partisanship), suggesting that ideological factions during the nonpartisan era may have provided some information to voters. They do find an important decrease in the power of incumbency in Minnesota after the switch to partisanship. Similarly, Ansolabehere and colleagues (2006) note a sharp increase in the correlation between votes for top-ballot offices and votes for state legislature in Minnesota upon the return to partisanship, indicating that the party labels helped to structure mass voting behavior.

There have been relatively few studies, however, of legislative behavior in Minnesota across the two eras. Mitau (1970) examined three issues in the 1950s and 60s on which the state parties had taken opposing stances and found relatively high cohesion among the legislature's ideological caucuses. Frederickson echoed these findings, noting that caucus cohesion was high on issues on which the national parties were polarized (cited in Mitau). Seitz and Shaw (1985, 154) examined all the contested votes in the 1971 state senate and found that "on over half of them the majority of Conservatives voted in exact opposition to the majority of Liberals." Fjelstad (1955, 361) agreed:

An analysis of the voting on all measures considered during the 1953 session satisfies the writer that Minnesota legislators tend to follow their factional commitments in much the same way that lawmakers in a partisan legislature respect their party lines.

Manning (2004) explored the differences in legislative activity across both eras and found that the state legislature saw a sharp drop in the number of laws passed per session after the return to partisanship. Brandt (1977) used interest group evaluations of legislators, as I do, finding that legislative partisanship was already on the upswing prior to the introduction of parties to the legislature, although his study was limited to just a few sessions.

ACCIDENTAL NONPARTISANSHIP

As mentioned previously, Minnesota and Nebraska are the only two US states to have utilized nonpartisan ballots in the selection of state legislators. The two states differ greatly, however, in their approaches toward this goal. Nebraska adopted nonpartisanship in the 1930s by popular initiative. While the idea of a nonpartisan, unicameral legislature had been championed by US Senator George Norris (R-NE), it only became a reality with the assent of Nebraska voters, who gave the initiative strong majorities all across the state (Masket and Shor 2015).

By contrast, Minnesota's decision to abandon parties in state legislative elections was made by the legislators themselves and appears to have been quite inadvertent, largely a result of the cross-cutting temperance issue. The chain of events began with a 1913 legislative proposal to require nonpartisan elections in municipal and judicial elections, a common proposal throughout the Progressive states in the early 20th century. A group of conservative Republicans led by state senator A. J. Rockne of Zumbrota opposed this, however, and sought to stop the bill by attaching a poison-pill amendment mandating nonpartisanship in state legislative elections, as well. Much to their surprise, the bill still passed both houses due to an odd confluence of political agendas. Conservative legislators saw the nonpartisan, top-two primary as a means of marginalizing the rising Socialist Party, while also a potential boon to their efforts to win reelection among their German and Scandinavian Republican constituents without being tied to their nominally "dry" party. Progressives, meanwhile, saw the new ballot as a way of undermining the established major parties. Liquor industry lobbyists saw the move to nonpartisanship as a way to break "dry" conservatives' lock on the legislature (Manning 2005; Seitz and Shaw 1985; Straumanis 1994).

Unlike Nebraska's embrace of nonpartisanship, which occurred after a multiyear public campaign, Minnesota's happened quite rapidly and nearly silently. According to Adrian (1952b, 161), "The Minnesota legislature had become nonpartisan without a single word of debate on the merits of the question." Newspaper editorials weighed in across the state, many expressing bewilderment. The *Red Wing Daily Republican* claimed that the nonpartisan legislature "was a suggestion so new and so radical that even the members who voted for it hardly realized what a revolutionary change" it was (quoted in Adrian 1952b, 161). Charles Cheney of the *Minneapolis Journal* expressed concern that "the Minnesota plan throws the door open to nominations of the liquor and other interests. They find it easy to juggle the contests, once these have degenerated into mere personal struggles" (quoted in Adrian 1952b, 162).

The factional patterns in the legislature remained somewhat ephemeral for several decades after the adoption of nonpartisanship. Leavitt (1977) reports that the legislature was largely divided between Progressives and Conservatives until the early 1930s, although the wet-dry split dominated business between 1912 and 1919. Additionally, a coalition of Non-Partisan Leaguers and Socialists formed the Farmer-Labor caucus by 1923, eventually becoming a prominent major group in the chamber. At least early on in this era, it was not uncommon for members to switch from one caucus to another if they thought their switch would place them in the majority faction, although this usually happened only when the factions were of comparable size (Leavitt 1977).

By the late 1930s, however, two dominant and enduring ideological factions had emerged within the Minnesota legislature, the Liberals and the Conservatives. Although these labels appeared on no ballots, it was widely known in state political circles that these factions, by the 1950s, affiliated strongly with the Democrat Farmer Labor Party (DFL)[1] and the Republican Party, respectively. These factions were reported to be stable over time (Mitau 1970), and they took on the roles played by legislative parties in other chambers, as well:

> Minnesota's legislators come to St. Paul without being bound to any party or officially committed to any platform. They appear to surrender much of their independence in a hurry, however. Members of both the House and the Senate divide into two factions,

1. The Farmer-Labor Party and the Democratic Party of Minnesota formally merged in April of 1944.

Conservative and Liberal, in the selection of presiding officers. It is
no secret that these divisions are coming because factional leaders
in each house often meet in advance of the session to agree upon
candidates for legislative offices. (Fjelstad 1955, 360)

Leavitt (1977) found the Liberal caucus to be the more disciplined
one, with members meeting more frequently to recommend voting positions on a wide range of issues. Conversely, reports Brandt (1977, 212),
"A freshman Conservative legislator was given to understand that the
party expected his vote on the selection of a speaker and the adoptions
of rules; otherwise, he was free to vote as he saw fit." Leavitt also notes
that independent-minded members of the Liberal caucus were occasionally challenged by DFLers in subsequent primaries, while straying
Conservatives were rarely disciplined. Nonetheless, each caucus maintained strict control over the floor when it held the majority. Fjelstad's
analysis of the 1953 session demonstrates that the statehouse speaker, a
Conservative, appointed Conservative chairmen and vice-chairmen to
all 39 standing legislative committees. Additionally, legislative leaders of
both factions actively recruited new candidates who pledged their support to their respective factional leaders.

What the Minnesota legislature has, therefore, is a legislative "party"
system in which the majority "party" manages the machinery of
lawmaking through the well-known instrumentalities of party
control—selection of presiding officers, naming of committee
chairmen, assignment of members to committees in sufficient
numbers to control them, majority and minority leaders, caucuses
and party discipline in voting. (Fjelstad 1955, 361)

In addition to their organization within the legislature, the caucuses
maintained cordial relations with the more formal state parties. Many
legislators were active in their respective state parties before running
for the legislature (challenging Adrian's [1952a] claim that there would
be a segregation between partisan and nonpartisan career paths). The

DFL regularly offered preprimary endorsements of legislative candidates aligned with Labor (*Winona Daily News* 1970b). Additionally, article 6, section 6 of the DFL's constitution stipulated that "Liberal members of the state legislature may be certified by the Credentials Committee as non-voting members of the state convention." Thus the DFL's own charter acknowledged Liberal legislators as tantamount to party members. As Fjelstad (1955, 363) adds, "Liberals are presumed to belong to the DFL while none of the Conservatives are, not even those who may be DFL outside the legislature." By 1971, veteran legislators were complaining about the intensity of partisanship within the ostensibly nonpartisan chamber (Seitz and Shaw 1985).

To get a sense of the level of polarization within the Minnesota legislature of the late nonpartisan period, I have collected a complete set of roll call votes from one legislative session. Figure 5.1 charts the first- and second-dimension "ideal points" (estimations of the preferences of legislators based on their roll call voting behavior) for members of the

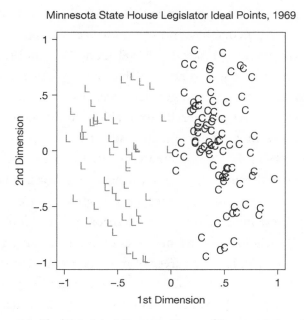

Figure 5.1 Ideal Points in Minnesota House of Representatives, 1969.

Minnesota House of Representatives in 1969. Members are labeled by their affiliated caucus: L for Liberals and C for Conservatives.

As the figure shows, Liberals and Conservatives are well sorted along the first (main) dimension of voting. Every Liberal is to the left of every Conservative. What's more, there are very few members located in the middle of the spectrum, with members clustered rather toward their coalitions' more extreme positions. Voting in this chamber is basically one-dimensional—cut-lines are overwhelmingly clustered around the 90-degree mark—and appears even more starkly divided than the US House of Representatives of that same era. And yet members were adhering to "party" labels that didn't even appear on the ballot.

What was it that drove the caucuses during the nonpartisan era? Was it simply an acknowledgment that a partyless chamber couldn't function well, and that only through some semblance of legislative partisanship could legislators achieve their career goals (Aldrich 1995; Schwartz 1989)? No doubt such incentives played some role here, although it should be noted that members of other nonpartisan chambers, such as Nebraska's Unicam through much of its history and the California Assembly during cross-filing (1914–59), not to mention the vast majority of city councils and county governments, have proven quite comfortable with disorganized legislative voting (Masket 2009; Welch and Carlson 1973).

In the case of Minnesota, it appears that the legislative caucuses were sustained by close ties with organized interests outside the chamber. Factional interest groups generally were able to unite along party lines to become active in elections and to lobby the legislature (Hathaway and Gieske 1985). Labor unions maintained strong pressure on members of the Liberal caucus to follow through on labor agenda items in the postwar era, and business interests pressured Conservative members to resist these items. Otto F. Christianson, the lead lobbyist for the Minnesota Association of Commerce and Industry during the 1950s and 60s, for example, made a career of monitoring pro-labor legislation authored by Liberals and pressuring Conservatives to oppose it (Mitau 1970, 110–13). Representatives of organized labor, meanwhile, while once wary of involvement within the party system, grew closely involved with

the DFL in the postwar era and advocated the election of Liberal legislators. Indeed, "Critics evince considerable alarm at the burgeoning power
of organized labor within the DFL and the Liberal caucus of the house"
(115–16). The Minnesota Farm Bureau also held "potent influence" over
Conservative legislators on a number of issues related to agriculture (119),
while the Farmers Union "makes no secret of its generally strong support
of the DFL and the Liberal caucus" (122). Some of the strongest factional
legislative divisions in this era occurred over labor and agricultural issues
(Brandt 1977, 211).

The tie between the Liberals and the labor movement is additionally
evidenced by labor's backing of efforts to reinstate party designations
in the chamber. While voters were wildly inconsistent in their feelings
regarding nonpartisanship in the state (Mitau 1960, 96–97), organized
labor and Liberals had been advocating it throughout the 1950s and 60s.
The Minnesota chapter of Americans for Democratic Action notably
backed party labels in 1969, 1971, and 1973, when it finally became law.

Clean-government advocates like the League of Women Voters and
various political scientists and newspaper editorial boards additionally
agitated for party labels throughout this time, viewing party affiliation
as a useful piece of information for voters in a low-information electoral
environment (*Winona Daily News* 1970c; 1971). For labor, however, the
effort had a more strategic purpose. Many political observers of the time
felt that nonpartisanship was helping to keep Conservatives in charge of
the statehouse. Throughout the postwar era, after all, the DFL had been
largely successful in electing gubernatorial and US senatorial candidates
statewide, and surveys showed that the DFL had a substantial plurality in
voter preferences, even while Conservatives had maintained majorities in
the state legislature (Hathaway and Gieske 1985; Manning 2005). It was
plausibly reasoned that this was a result of left-leaning voters unwittingly
supporting Conservative legislative candidates due to nonpartisan balloting. Indeed, Elazar, Gray, and Spano (1999) demonstrate that some very
left-leaning districts were voting for Conservative candidates at this time.

For the same reasons, the DFL strongly lobbied for partisan elections
throughout the 1950s and 60s. The Republican Party wavered somewhat

in its support, although Conservatives in the statehouse never supported partisan balloting to the degree that Liberals did. By 1970, Republicans had come out firmly against partisanship, no doubt realizing that continued Conservative control of the legislature lay in the balance (Seitz and Shaw 1985; *Winona Daily News* 1970a).

While party designation bills had been introduced throughout the 1950s and 60s, one did not pass until 1973, when, for the first time in state history, the Liberal caucus took control of the legislature under a DFL governor.[2] Around the time of its adoption, Liberal and Conservative legislators took on the designations of DFL and IR (Independent Republican), respectively, in official legislative records.[3] They wouldn't run on partisan ballots until 1974, however, and thus the first fully partisan state house was seated in 1975. The state senate, elected in staggered four-year terms, didn't become fully partisan until 1977.

METHODS, MEASUREMENTS, AND EXPECTATIONS

Much of the literature on partisanship and nonpartisanship suggests there should be important changes in legislative behavior once members were elected on a partisan ballot. Specifically, the electoral connection should compel legislators to hew closer to their party lines. Running on a party ticket should make centrist behavior potentially more costly. Thus we should expect to see greater legislative partisanship under partisan elections.

Minnesota, however, may provide a special case, in which ideological caucuses were already behaving much like formal legislative parties long before the electoral connection existed. In this framework, the move to partisan elections was a mere formality; strong parties had already

2. Interestingly, the surge in Liberal vote shares came prior to the reintroduction of party labels, largely because of court-mandated redistrictings that benefited urban constituencies in the wake of *Baker* v. *Carr* (1966).

3. The switch from ideological coalitions to formal parties was a nearly seamless one. Of those legislators identifying themselves as Liberals in 1971, all but one identified with the DFL in 1973. Similarly, all but one of the self-identified Conservatives in 1971 claimed membership in the Republican Party in 1973.

functionally existed in the legislature for some time. Thus the expectations are unclear; the parties' literature predicts greater legislative partisanship under partisan elections, while a review of the peculiar history of
Minnesota would predict no real change.

Legislative partisanship, of course, comes in a variety of flavors. I examine two of them in this chapter. The first aspect of polarization I examine is the phenomenon of the parties moving further apart from each
other. Thus I seek to measure *interparty ideological distance*—the mean
difference between the parties. Another form of polarization involves
the parties becoming more internally cohesive, with copartisans voting
in lockstep with one another. Thus I also measure *intraparty ideological
cohesiveness*. Notably, one form of polarization may occur in the absence
of the other, although the two typically move together.

To measure these trends, I have collected legislator ratings from two
left-leaning interest groups, the AFL-CIO and Americans for Democratic
Action (ADA) from 1969 to 1989.[4] In choosing time periods and groups,
I was somewhat at the mercy of the available data; the state legislature
maintains copies of these and other interest group publications, but the
collections of the AFL-CIO and the ADA cover the relevant years and
have by far the most sessions available.

Interest group ratings of legislators are admittedly inferior measures
of legislators' "ideal points" when compared to item response methods
that consider every roll call cast in a session. Not only are interest group
ratings derived from smaller numbers of votes, but those votes are hardly
randomly selected; they are on the issues that the interest group consid-
ers most important. All these things can somewhat distort perceptions
of legislator preferences. There are two mitigating factors here: First,
I have used two interest groups rather than one, allowing for a much
broader range of issues on which legislators are evaluated.[5] Second, these

4. These files were graciously made available by Robbie LaFleur, director of the Minnesota
Legislative Reference Library.
5. The two group's scores are similar (they correlate at .79) but not identical. As Brandt (1977,
216) notes, "Liberalism, as defined by the ADA, is by no means identical to liberalism, as
defined by the AFL-CIO."

Table 5.1 AVAILABILITY OF MINNESOTA
INTEREST GROUP SCORES BY YEAR

	ADA	AFL-CIO
1969	✓	
1971	✓	
1973	✓	
1975	✓	✓
1977	✓	✓
1978		✓
1980		✓
1981		✓
1983		✓
1985	✓	
1987	✓	
1988	✓	
1989	✓	

particular interest groups chose a wide range of votes (at least 25 per session on several different issues).

I have limited my analysis to the 134 members of the Minnesota House of Representatives, as the staggered nature of senators' terms presents further challenges to the analysis. Unfortunately, ratings for both interest groups were not available for all years during this time span. Table 5.1 lists the years available for each. Where both years are available, I have averaged the scores. To make sure these scores were comparable across years, I have adjusted them using the Stata "inflat".do file created by Jeffrey Lewis (Groseclose, Levitt, and Snyder 1999).[6] The resulting scores are scaled from 0 to 100, with 100 being the most liberal position. Scores may occasionally exceed 100 due to inflation transformations. These scores correlate with first-dimension W-NOMINATE at −.673 in 1969, suggesting a reasonably strong fit with more complete roll call records.

6. The file is available at http://www.sscnet.ucla.edu/polisci/faculty/lewis/#a_software.

The analysis used here is essentially a regression discontinuity (RD) model. RD models are useful when trying to distinguish a specific effect from a more general one. For example, suppose we are trying to determine the effect of an academic merit award on a student's future educational success. It can be difficult to measure this effect if that merit award is given out based on previous academic success; is later success attributable to the award itself, or to general academic prowess? An RD model avoids this problem by just focusing on those cases immediately above and below the "treatment" threshold. That is, in the education example, students just below the award threshold are presumably quite intellectually similar to those just above the threshold; we can then see whether receiving the award has any independent contribution to later successes (Thistlethwaite and Campbell 1960).

In this case, we are interested in distinguishing the immediate effect of the switch to partisan balloting from other roughly contemporaneous trends. These other trends are legion. Court-mandated redistrictings substantially helped urban Liberal candidates in the early 1970s, allowing the Liberals to take over the state legislature in 1973 for the first time in decades. Additionally, the legislature moved from biennial to annual legislative sessions in 1973, as well. Finally, we know there has been a secular increase in legislative partisanship at the national level and in many states since the 1970s. All these things make it difficult to sort out the exact causes of any increases in legislative partisanship beginning in 1975. Nonetheless, the literature on legislative parties suggests that any sharp increase in party-line voting would be most credibly attributed to the switch to partisan elections.

RESULTS

Figure 5.2 displays the histograms of legislator interest group ratings by year, with conservative members on the left and liberals on the right. The main lesson from this figure is that polarization does occur over time; the distributions are largely unimodal (indicating a tendency toward moderation) in the earlier graphs but become quite bimodal (indicating

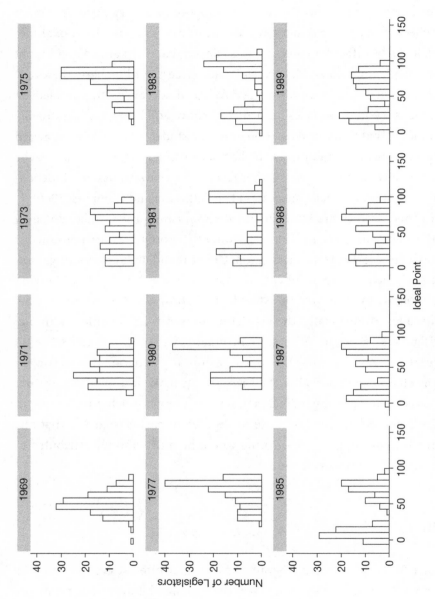

Figure 5.2 Histograms of Interest Group Ratings of Minnesota Legislators, 1969–89.

a tendency toward extremism) in the latter ones. However, we don't see a sharp bimodal pattern emerge until 1980. These were the legislators elected in 1978, the third partisan legislative election of the decade.

A similar trend can be detected in Figure 5.3, which plots out the interest group scores for each state house member from 1969 to 1989, with DFLers (Liberals from 1969 to 1973) appearing as hollow dots and Republicans (Conservatives from 1969 to 1973) appearing as plusses. Lowess trendlines run through each party's data points, with separate trendlines estimated for the nonpartisan era (1969–73) and the partisan era (1975–89). One thing that this figure shows is that there was considerable polarization prior to the partisan ballots. The typical Liberal voted well to the left of the typical Conservative. Additionally, as in Figure 5.2, a sharp increase in party cohesion can be detected in the early 1980s: While the earlier years demonstrate considerable ideological overlap between the parties, the parties have neatly segregated by the 1980s, with nearly every DFLer to the left of every Republican.

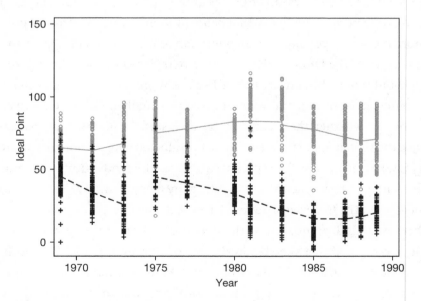

Figure 5.3 Interest Group Ratings for Minnesota Legislators by Year and Party. NOTES: Solid blue circles indicate Liberals (1969-73) and DFL members (1975-89). Hollow red dots indicate Conservatives (1969-73) and Independent Republicans (1975-89). Trend lines are lowess lines calculated by party for each era.

The trendlines in Figure 5.3 do show a general trend toward polariza-tion, but there does not appear to be a sharp increase at the time that the chamber moved to partisan elections. Indeed, it appears that the chamber was heading in a more polarized direction in the early 1970s, with Conservatives, in particular, moving more toward the ideological extremes, but the shift to partisan elections coincided with the rise of a more moderate group of Republicans. The DFLers, meanwhile, appear no more liberal in 1975 than the Liberals did in 1973, continuing the same slow, steady trend toward polarization.

What accounts for the increase in polarization in the early 1980s? Was it an infusion of newer, more partisan members, or did the veteran legislators polarize by themselves? An examination of the available data shows that both occurred. Of the 133 members who served in 1975, 47 were still in office in 1981. Those veteran DFLers, on average, shifted their interest group ratings by 10 points in the liberal direction, while veteran Independent Republicans moved 17 points in the conservative direction. The DFL as a whole, meanwhile, became 18 points more liberal over the same time period, while the Independent Republicans became 18 points more conservative. Thus both conversion and replacement appear to be at play here. The DFLers who retired were replaced by more liberal fresh-men, but those who stayed in office became more liberal, as well, and both Republican freshman and veterans became equally more conservative.

To test whether there was a detectable shift in polarization patterns with the switch to partisan elections, I conducted a regression discontinu-ity analysis using the "RD" package in Stata. The model simply examines shifts in members' interest group ratings by party, using 1975 as the treat-ment year. The first row of Table 5.2 shows the results. Among Democrats, there was a 4.1 point shift in the liberal direction at this point in time. However, given that the standard error of this shift is 4.3, this result is statistically indistinguishable from zero. Among Republicans, there was an impressive 27.1 point shift—a statistically significant result ($p \leq .001$)—but it was in the *liberal direction*.

An analysis of mean interest group ratings for legislators suggests that there was no real increase in interparty ideological distance associated

Table 5.2 REGRESSION DISCONTINUITY ANALYSIS

	DFL (Liberals)	Republicans (Conservatives)
Mean interest group scores	4.11	27.10***
	(4.32)	(4.81)
Standard deviation of interest group scores	−6.35***	−6.42***
	(1.39)	(1.95)

NOTE: The cell entries above are regression discontinuity coefficients measuring shifts in legislators' interest group scores by party at the treatment year, 1975—the point at which party labels were introduced. Higher numbers indicate more liberal voting behavior. Standard errors appear in parentheses.

with the adoption of party designations on the ballots. In Figure 5.4, however, I plot out the standard deviation of ideal points by party (and for the entire chamber) by year. Even if the parties didn't move further apart from each other, that is, it is possible that they became more internally cohesive with the adoption of party labels. The standard deviation of interest group scores should capture this.

As Figure 5.4 shows, both parties experienced a rise in intraparty ideological diversity in 1973, but then the standard deviations began to drop after the adoption of party labels in 1975. The scores spiked again in the early 1980s, although the Republicans again became more internally cohesive thereafter, while the DFL remained somewhat more diverse. Meanwhile, the overall chamber saw a greater diversity of views in the 1980s, consistent with ideological polarization shown in Figures 5.2 and 5.3. The patterns in Figure 5.4 are consistent with the idea that the adoption of party designations induced greater internal cohesion among the parties.

I test this in the second row of Table 5.2, again using the regression discontinuity model. In this case, both parties show statistically significant results, with the switch to party labels in 1975 associated with a more than 6 point drop in the standard deviation of interest group ratings. An important caveat here, however, is that this shift is highly sensitive to 1973's unusually high standard deviations. When 1973 is removed, both parties' results lose their statistical significance.

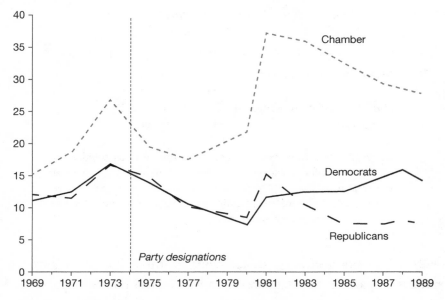

Figure 5.4 Standard Deviations of Interest Group Ratings, by Party and Year.

DISCUSSION

In the above analysis, I examined two possible forms of legislative polarization in the Minnesota state house: interparty ideological distance and intraparty ideological cohesion. The legislative roll call evidence suggested that the ideological distance between the parties increased steadily over time between the 1960s and the 1980s but saw no sharp increase around the time of the switch to partisan elections in 1975. There was, however, a measurable and statistically significant drop in the standard deviation of interest group scores within each party concurrent with the switch to partisan elections. Thus at least one form of legislative polarization increased at this critical juncture, although it may well be an artifact of unusually high intraparty diversity in 1973.

All in all, the evidence for a rise in legislative partisanship with the switch to partisan elections is somewhat paltry. The reason for this is not that Minnesota never really embraced legislative partisanship; on the contrary, it already had it well before the switch to partisan elections.

The Conservative and Liberal ideological caucuses in the Minnesota state house had, by the 1960s, taken on the roles of modern legislative parties, organizing chamber rules, determining committee leadership, structuring the legislative agenda, and pressuring members on roll call votes. As in cross-filing California and nonpartisan Nebraska, several decades of nonpartisanship eventually gave way to partisan behavior by legislators.

Why did nonpartisanship ultimately fail in Minnesota? It's certainly possible that, to some extent, members saw the value of collective action and recognized that membership in a long coalition would yield greater ideological and career payoffs than independence would. More plausibly and immediately, though, the partisan legislative activity in the Minnesota of the 1950s and 60s appears to derive from the interplay between Minnesota's legislative caucuses and the state's interest groups. That is, legislators behaved as partisans because policy demanders demanded it. As described in this chapter, by the 1950s, the state's interest groups were strongly polarized along traditional party lines, and their activity in elections and their lobbying patterns in the statehouse helped to maintain strong discipline among the ideological caucuses. Business groups strongly backed Conservative legislators, while labor unions rallied behind Liberals. Direct evidence of this interplay is scant today, but it seems reasonable to conclude that the legislators that benefited from these groups' largesse recognized the value of that support and did what was necessary to continue to earn it: they voted with their coalition.

Policy demanders, it seems, are influential enough over legislators to enforce party discipline even in the absence of an informed electorate. They were so successful in Minnesota that switching to formal partisan elections was little more than a formality, a post hoc ratification of the switch that had already occurred.

6

The California Recall

"A Sprint with No Primary"

Statewide political races rarely capture the attention of the nation, no less the world. But in 2003, California captured both when its residents recalled twice-elected governor Gray Davis (D) and replaced him with film action hero Arnold Schwarzenegger (R). Only the second gubernatorial recall election in American history,[1] the relatively quick two-month election cycle commanded the attention of journalists and public officials across the country.

Among the recall election's many quirks was that the replacement election occurred simultaneously. According to the state constitution, the recall ballot consists of exactly two questions: shall the official be recalled, and who shall replace him or her. California is one of just six states of the 19 that allow recalls that have such simultaneous elections. One of the things that makes California's system particularly unusual is the very low threshold for candidate entry in recall elections: 65 signatures plus a $3500 filing fee. There is no primary election, no official caucus or convention procedure, no state-sanctioned way for a party to choose its nominee for this election. Thus the California ballot was filled with multiple candidates from each party—135 candidates in all.

---

1. North Dakota Governor Lynn Frazier was recalled in 1921. A third recall attempt would occur in Wisconsin in 2012, when Governor Scott Walker survived a recall election.

As I will discuss in this chapter, these recall provisions, written into state codes in the early 1910s, were part of a Progressive-era attempt to undermine the major political parties. This reform fits well with the others examined in the book. We see not only a reform designed to undermine parties, but party adaptation to the reform. As the 2003 example demonstrates, the parties are able to functionally nominate their candidates even when they are deprived of official means of doing so. Indeed, by election day, despite widespread fears of a dispersed vote and the new governor taking office with just 5 or 10 percent of the vote, just three candidates split 94 percent of the vote, with Schwarzenegger winning the election by a near majority. This, as we shall see, was no accident; the parties were quite active in winnowing candidates and reducing voters' choices.

The evidence I draw from in this chapter is both qualitative and quantitative. I interviewed a number of journalists, activists, and political consultants in the Sacramento area in 2006 and 2007, both in person and over the phone. I have also conducted an analysis of campaign donation patterns in the 2003 race and those that immediately preceded it. I begin by explaining the background and details of the recall, and then describe the two parties' responses to it, which were quite different from each other. Both had the effect of serving as de facto primaries, with the parties converging around single candidates and working to drive others from the races.

THE RECALL AS ANTIPARTY DEVICE

The recall was broadly advocated by Progressive reformers in the early 1900s and was often instituted alongside the other major Progressive reforms of the initiative and the referendum. While hardly invented by the Progressives—recall provisions can be traced back to western state Populists, 19th-century Switzerland, the Articles of Confederation, the Roman Republic, and ancient Athens (Cronin 1989)—the early 20th century was the first time it saw widespread use at the state and local level. It first came into broad use in California in the wake of a 1902 constitutional amendment that allowed municipal governments to experiment with different governing systems via the initiative process. Some cities, including Los Angeles and San Francisco, adopted the recall, and reformers used this new tool to drive some corrupt public officials from office (Mowry 1951). The state would adopt the recall for state officials in 1911, becoming only the second state to do so[2] (Oregon had adopted it in 1908). The recall has become a popular tool in American politics; some 5,000 or so recalls have been held, the vast majority at the level of city council or school board. There have been fewer than 40 state legislative recalls (nearly half since 2010), and only three gubernatorial ones (Weinstein 2005).

To categorize the recall as a specifically antiparty reform would be incomplete. To be sure, it was enacted in many states, including California, as part of the overall Progressive agenda, and was seen, along with the initiative and the referendum, as a way for citizens to take some control over state politics away from the parties, widely seen as corrupt institutions. The general theme of the recall and other Progressive reforms, writes Hofstadter (1955, 5–6),

> was the effort to restore a type of economic individualism and political democracy that was widely believed to have existed earlier in America and to have been destroyed by the great corporation and the corrupt party machine; and with that restoration to bring back a kind of morality and civic purity that was also believed to have been lost.

And the recall was used in California to threaten politicians who appeared to be under the influence of and benefiting from graft provided by local political machines (Persily 1997).

And yet California's own approach to the recall, involving the simultaneous replacement election with no primary, wasn't necessarily intended to undermine parties. Indeed, it was devised before primaries were even in

2. The recall was a highly controversial measure when first considered in California, particularly when Governor Hiram Johnson proposed applying it to judges. Conservative Republicans argued that it would make judges more political by requiring them to "keep their ears to the ground," but Johnson responded that this was preferable to them keeping their ears to the railroad tracks (a reference to the power of the railroad lobby) (Bean and Rawls 1983).

widespread use. Nonetheless, regardless of its Progressive authors' intent, California's recall and replacement procedures seemed to be a perfect tool for undermining the political parties. If officeholders had previously marched to the party's tune regardless of voters' concerns, they could now no longer do that—just the appearance of being under the party's thumb could result in that officeholder being recalled. And the simultaneous and primaryless replacement election ensured that the party could not dominate the outcome of the recall and install another party person. With no convention or primary to consolidate the party vote, any efforts by the party to limit the people's choices for a replacement candidate would be futile. Low barriers to the ballot would ensure that the people would have a wide range of candidates from which to choose, even from within the same party.

While California is one of 19 states that allow recalls, and one of six that have a simultaneous, primaryless replacement election, some features of candidate entry make the state unique.[3] The state has one of the lowest signature thresholds for a recall election, with 12 percent of the number of voters from the previous statewide election being required to qualify the election (Cronin 1989). It additionally has an unusually low candidate entry threshold for recalls, requiring gubernatorial replacement candidates to secure 65 signatures and pay a $3500 filing fee. These requirements are lower than for traditional statewide races (Hershey 2013). These aspects of California's recall system conspire to undermine parties; recalls may appear with little warning. And the low candidate entry threshold means that the parties do not hold a monopoly on access to the ballot; *many* state residents can amass 65 signatures and pay $3500, as the events of 2003 would demonstrate.

A SETTING FOR RECALL

Despite his narrow reelection in 2002, Democratic governor Gray Davis quickly found himself facing public criticism and voters' wrath. The recession of 2001–2 hit California hard, producing a $38 billion budget

3. http://www.ncsl.org/research/elections-and-campaigns/recall-of-state-officials.aspx.

shortfall that jeopardized many longstanding Democratic social pro-
grams. An effort to balance the budget by tripling automobile license fees
managed to anger both wealthy and poorer Californians. A simultaneous
energy crisis resulted in drastic increases in resident's energy bills and
periodic rolling blackouts, for which many blamed Davis. By the spring of
2003, Davis found himself with a 24 percent approval rating.

Antitax activist Ted Costa helped organize the Davis Recall Committee
in February of that year, promptly beginning signature gathering efforts
that were advertised heavily on conservative talk radio. It would be a
stretch to call this recall a Republican Party tactic; it was not organized or
endorsed by many party insiders, at least not at first, although its initial
instigators were nearly all Republicans. Indeed, the recall was initially
interpreted by many as a distraction by a fringe group, much like prior
gubernatorial recall attempts.

A recall petition has been circulated against nearly every California
governor since 1911. Prior to 2003, however, none had come close to securing a spot on the ballot. What made this year different was the pledge
in May by US Rep. Darrell Issa (R-San Diego) to donate millions of his
own dollars to help in the signature gathering effort. California's sophisticated petition signature industry quickly put this money to good use,
and on July 23, the secretary of state certified that the recall campaign had
collected 1.4 million valid signatures, well beyond the 897,158 required.
Under state rules requiring a prompt election, the recall election would
be held on October 7, just 76 days later. The campaign was to be, in the
words of Schwarzenegger campaign aid Patrick Dorinson, "a sprint with
no primary."

THE REPUBLICAN RESPONSE: COORDINATION

I have detailed the Republican approach to the recall in a separate article
(Masket 2011) but will summarize the findings here. The recall presented
both opportunity and danger for the state Republican Party. The opportunity lay in the fact that given Democrats' voter registration advantage

and the tendency for the GOP primary process to produce very conservative nominees, Republicans weren't likely to take the governor's mansion by conventional means any time soon. Indeed, they had just lost the 2002 governor's race to an unpopular Democratic incumbent during both a recession and an energy crisis. And their party had controlled the state legislature for only two of the previous thirty years. The recall offered a way to allow a moderate, popular Republican to seize the governor's office.

The risks, however, were significant, in that the provisions of the state recall allowed for no formal party coordination method. Anyone who reached the state's modest filing requirements would appear on the ballot. And the Republican Party had no shortage of ambitious, wealthy politicians who might consider running. This coordination problem threatened to jeopardize this unusual opportunity. Even if the majority of voters were willing to support Republicans, the high number of candidates could split the conservative vote and throw the election back to the Democrats.

Republican elites responded to this scenario by largely rallying behind Arnold Schwarzenegger. For some, this was a difficult move. Schwarzenegger was notably to the left of much of the party's leadership, having embraced rights for same-sex couples, environmental regulations, and modest gun control. Schwarzenegger had considered running for governor in 2002 but faced some strong initial pushback from within his party, making it seem that winning the Republican nomination might be possible, but would be challenging and costly both to his wallet and to the positive public image he'd spent decades crafting.

The move to have Republicans embrace Schwarzenegger in 2003 was led by a small group of relatively moderate insiders, many of whom had been close advisors to previous Republican governor Pete Wilson. These advisors included Wilson aide Bob White, political consultant George Gorton, Republican Party chair Shawn Steel, Republican media consultant Don Sipple, and former gubernatorial spokesperson Larry Thomas. In a private meeting, Wilson made it clear to Schwarzenegger that if he wanted to run, "the people around this table could help him set up a fund-raising network and find people to teach him the issues" (Mathews 2006, 69).

These party insiders reached out to more conservative forces, including state county chairs, the formal state party apparatus, local conservative activists, prominent donors, and others, and largely found that partisans were willing to put aside their particular issues and rally behind the moderate Schwarzenegger to seize this rare opportunity. As Schwarzenegger media consultant Rob Stutzman said,

> Nothing cures ideological purity like losing a couple elections. So [party insiders] saw, in Arnold, the opportunity to win and basically govern and have a place of primacy again politically for Republicans, no matter what kind of Republican he was. (Telephone interview with the author on December 27, 2007)

The next part was somewhat more difficult: convincing other Republican candidates to drop out.

The major candidates who posed a threat to Schwarzenegger solidifying the Republican vote were:

- Bill Simon, the Republican gubernatorial nominee in 2002;
- Peter Ueberroth, the former commissioner of Major League Baseball;
- Tom McClintock, a fiscally conservative state senator who had been the party's nominee for state controller the previous year.

This is not to ignore a number of other prominent candidates, such as moderate former Los Angeles mayor Richard Riordan (who declined to run once he learned that his friend Schwarzenegger was in) and Rep. Issa (who dropped out early). But it was primarily Simon, Ueberroth, and McClintock who remained in the race after the initial announcements.

The pressure applied to each of them came in a variety of forms. The formal Republican Party of California issued an endorsement—rare for that party up until that time—for Schwarzenegger in late September. Party officials called the candidates and gave press conferences urging them to drop out. A variety of key conservative endorsements from the Orange County Lincoln Club and the widow of Proposition 13 architect Howard Jarvis collectively sent the message that conservatives were accepting Schwarzenegger.

Donations themselves played an important role in communicating the broader party message. Schwarzenegger raised money very effectively and steadily, commanding some $20 million in just two months' time. But the others found their fundraising efforts anemic, especially compared to past efforts.

One way of examining campaign finance patterns in 2003 is to compare them to the previous cycle in 2002. There are convenient parallels between the Republican contests in both years. Both featured a range of candidates across different backgrounds and ideological positions. Each had a moderate (Schwarzenegger in 2003 and Riordan in 2002), a mainstream business Republican (Ueberroth in 2003 and Bill Jones in 2002), and a more traditional conservative (Bill Simon in both years). Figure 6.1 shows how funding transferred from one cycle to the next among donors who were active in both years. This analysis is limited to high-level donors who contributed at least $1000 in each cycle. Only transfers of more than

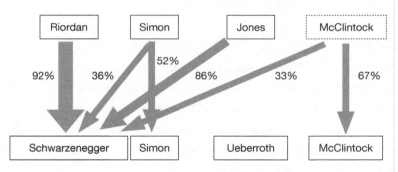

Figure 6.1 Republican Campaign Donation Patterns across 2002 and 2003.
NOTE: Top row consists of Republican candidates for governor in 2002, plus Tom McClintock, the Republican nominee for Controller. The bottom row consists of the four major Republican candidates for the recall replacement ballot in 2003. Arrows show the direction of funds among donors who contributed at least $1,000 in both 2002 and 2003. For example, 36% of those who donated to Simon in 2002 donated to Schwarzenegger in 2003. Transfers of 10% or less are not depicted.

10 percent are depicted. I have additionally included Tom McClintock, an iconoclastic conservative candidate in the recall and the Republican nominee for controller in 2002.

As can be seen, 92 percent of Riordan's multiyear donors in 2002 went on to donate to Schwarzenegger the next year. Moderate money stayed moderate. Bill Simon was able to retain only about half of his 2002 donors; 36 percent went on to donate to Schwarzenegger. Eighty-six percent of Jones's donors bled over to Schwarzenegger, as well. Only McClintock had much success in holding onto his donor base, but a third of his donors still bled over to Schwarzenegger.

This signal was hard for the candidates to miss; elite Republican money was going to Schwarzenegger. This is part of what led Bill Simon to conclude, "That wasn't really my time. I kind of felt like it was Arnold's time." Ueberroth similarly came to the conclusions that he couldn't win without cutting into Schwarzenegger's backing and couldn't figure out a realistic way to do that. Simon bowed out of the race in late August; Ueberroth followed a week later.

State senator Tom McClintock, however, proved more resistant to pleas that he leave the race. Many party officials, elected officials, and interest group leaders pressured McClintock, both publicly and privately, to bow out. As he explained in a later interview (Masket 2011):

> There were individuals contacting me, "worried about my political future," they said, and some sincere, some not very sincere. . . . Every day they'd have some functionary on the television saying, "If he doesn't get out of the race today, it'll be the end of his political career. He'll never be able to run for dog-catcher. We will recall him." There were all sorts of threats that were being conveyed through the public airwaves by party officials.

McClintock elected to remain in the race, however. Ultimately, he turned out to be not much of a threat to Schwarzenegger, securing only 13 percent to the actor's 49. But efforts to drive other, more moderate Republicans out of the race yielded considerable payoffs.

Schwarzenegger may well have won the race without any party activity. Even if no one had pressured Ueberroth, Simon, and others out of the race, he still might have proven popular enough to secure a plurality of the vote. But for one thing, that would have deprived him of considerable political capital upon taking office; he would have been seen as a fringe or joke candidate rather than the one who had nearly cleared a majority in a field of 135 candidates. For another, it was not obvious ex ante that a splitting of the Republican vote would have been harmless. Had three or four quality Republican candidates remained in the race while Democrats consolidated around one of their own, even a strongly pro-Republican electorate could have ended up with a Democratic replacement governor. It therefore made some difference what the Democrats were up to.

THE DEMOCRATS: A DEFECTION, FOLLOWED BY CONSOLIDATION

The Democrats' situation as the recall approached was similar to Republicans', in the sense that they also faced a substantial collective-action problem. The lack of a primary made it challenging to coordinate on a single candidate for the replacement ballot. And there were many potentially good candidates, including the state's two Democratic US senators, Barbara Boxer and Dianne Feinstein, who had both repeatedly won statewide contests. The presence of numerous strong candidates contributed to a prisoner's dilemma—any given candidate might see herself as winning, but the presence of many candidates making the same calculation would dilute the Democratic vote and potentially throw the election to the Republicans.

But Democrats faced their own particular wrinkles in addressing the recall. For one, there was the widespread belief, backed by some polling, that fielding any replacement candidate at all would make the recall of Governor Davis more likely to pass. If Democratic voters disenchanted with Governor Davis, that is, saw a plausible Democratic alternative on the ballot, they might be more likely to support the recall, whereas if they saw only Republicans and fringe candidates on the replacement ballot, they'd be more likely to view the recall as a partisan stunt and vote to keep Davis in office. This understanding ended up increasing pressure on ambitious Democratic politicians to stay out of the replacement race. But it also created rifts within the party. That is, those with greater loyalty to Governor Davis had a stronger incentive to stay out of the race, while those with longstanding grievances against him had a stronger incentive to jump in.

The decision to have no Democratic candidate was made and enforced by a coterie of party officials, officeholders, and allied interest group leaders. According to respondents, people including state Democratic chair Art Torres, California Federation of Labor president Art Pulaski, San Francisco mayor Willie Brown, attorney general Bill Lockyer, and state senate president John Burton contacted potential candidates and urged them to stay out of the race. "The Democratic elected establishment, the party establishment, had all come to the conclusions that they needed to keep the field clear so that the only question before the voters would be recall or don't recall," explains Democratic consultant Richie Ross.[4] In the words of Democratic consultant Ed Emerson, "80% of the California Democratic activists and maybe 90% of the California money said, 'Okay, nobody gets in.' You know, and that included Feinstein, Boxer, Pelosi— everybody. . . . It was, 'Do not get in this race at risk . . . of your political death.'"[5]

For a time, this united front appeared to hold. It was tested by state insurance commissioner John Garamendi, who briefly flirted with a run. As Democratic consultant Roger Salazar[6] explains,

> Garamendi . . . jumped into the race for about a day, and then got so much heat . . . especially from Labor, that he dropped out again. But yeah, John [Garamendi] announced . . . that he was gonna throw his hat into the ring. . . . And then again, over the weekend, he basically

4. Interview with author, December 13, 2013.
5. Interview with author, October 5, 2007.
6. Interview with author, October 5, 2007.

rescinded that and said, "No, no. I was just putting my name out there and seeing what's up. And then I took it back." And again, that from the way I understand it, it was Art Torres and the Labor leaders—you know, Art Pulaski from the Labor Fed and others who kind of basically went to John and put the screws to him, so to speak.

Garamendi ended up dropping out on August 9, just hours before the candidate filing deadline (Orlov 2003).

Prominent Democratic officeholders, including Senators Feinstein and Boxer, Rep. Nancy Pelosi, and Garamendi, gave public statements vowing they would not enter the race and participated in statewide advertising warning about the dangers of the recall (Ainsworth 2003). Yet the temptation to enter was particularly great for the state's Democratic lieutenant governor, Cruz Bustamante.

Bustamante had previously served as a state assemblyman from Fresno and was elected speaker of the assembly in 1996. He became lieutenant governor in 1998, becoming the first Latino elected statewide in California in over a century and the highest-ranking elected Latino in the United States. He also had a long-running quarrel with Gray Davis. While the two had been elected as a team in 1998, they disagreed sharply over the proper response to Proposition 187, an anti-undocumented-immigrant initiative passed by voters in 1994. Bustamante wanted the governor's office to file suit against the implementation of the initiative, but Davis demurred. The disagreement became very public, with Bustamante offering some sharp criticisms of Davis's stance. Allegedly in reprisal, Davis's office reclaimed nine capitol parking permits that had been held by Bustamante staffers. This dispute, simultaneously substantive and petty, served to undermine any loyalty Bustamante felt toward the struggling governor.

According to Ed Emerson, Davis more generally had a political management problem that created potential enemies for him within his own party: "He was unresponsive in terms of certain issues. He was someone who took a bow anytime he signed a bill, whether he had worked on the bill or whether he acknowledged the author or sponsored the bill or not." Another Democratic consultant described Davis as being a politician that used everyone around him: "Gray Davis said there were two types of people in politics, as far as he was concerned: useful and less useful."

But Bustamante's considerations went beyond a personal spat with the governor. As a man who'd gone from an appointed state legislator to second-in-command of the state in just five years, he'd harbored his own ambitions of becoming governor, and the recall simply made that easier. If he had to wait until 2006 to run in the open seat election, he'd have been competing against some very well-funded Democratic rivals in the primary, including attorney general Bill Lockyer, treasurer Phil Angelides, and controller Steve Westly. As Ed Emerson remarked, "Those sorts of folks were gonna get in, and it was gonna cost Cruz between $10 million and $20 million just to get a seat at the table which he's never been able to raise money. You know, he's always had a tougher time raising money than the other candidates." Consultant Richie Ross conceded, "He was never an extraordinary fundraiser." The recall election presented Bustamante with a quick way to avoid a costly primary.

When Bustamante began issuing statements that he was considering running, traditional Democratic allies immediately pushed back and publicly urged him not to enter. The pushback was "huge," says Emerson: "Everybody talked to him. I mean, Art Pulaski, the head of AFLCIO . . . the Building Trades, Jim Croab with the Pipefitters. . . . You know, basically the big Labor Unions—SEIU, AFSCME [were saying], 'Don't get in the race. Don't do this to us. . . . You're gonna screw the pooch here.'" Bustamante nonetheless entered the race.

Democratic leaders, stung by Bustamante's apostasy, struggled with the best ways to deal with the situation and arrive at the best possible outcome in the October election. As Figure 6.2 shows, at least at first, Bustamante's fundraising efforts were somewhat paltry. Bustamante raised approximately $47,000 per day during August—a rate that would seem impressive in a more typical election but left him wanting for the two-month recall campaign. Schwarzenegger was raising an average of $302,000 per day—more than six times Bustamante's pace.

As seen in the previous section, one of things that helped Schwarzenegger's campaign was the fact that so many facets of the GOP backed

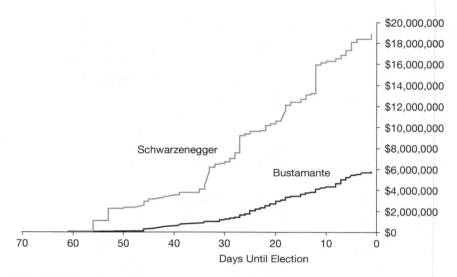

Figure 6.2 Fundraising by Bustamante and Schwarzenegger in 2003 Recall.

him, as revealed in campaign finance data; those who had been active in previous Republican primary contests converged on Schwarzenegger, even many of those who had backed far more conservative candidates. What kind of success did Bustamante have in commanding the support of previously active Democratic donors? To test this question, I have examined the contributions to all Democratic candidates in the three contested statewide party primaries in 1998 (attorney general, insurance commissioner, and governor) and in 2002 (secretary of state, insurance commissioner, and controller). I then limited the analysis to those donors who contributed in at least five of the six contests and donated an average of at least $5000 per contest. I dub these individuals "elite donors."

Only 35 donors meet this elite status. A list of them, along with their donation information for the recall, can be seen in Table 6.1. Of the 35 elite Democratic donors, only 21 contributed in the recall. Of those, 13 contributed directly to Bustamante, with others giving to a variety of committees opposing the recall and some contributing just to Governor Davis's antirecall campaign. (Notably, five gave to Schwarzenegger.) Only five of these 36 elite donors contributed to Bustamante prior to September 2003. By comparison, a similar analysis of 26 elite Republican donors finds

Table 6.1 ELITE DEMOCRATIC DONORS AND THEIR ACTIVITY IN RECALL

Donor	Recipient(s)	Days after recall certified that donor gave to Bustamante
Anheuser-Busch	Schwarzenegger, antirecall campaign	N/A
AT&T	Bustamante, antirecall campaign	69
Auburn Manor Holding Corp	Bustamante, antirecall campaign	29
Cabazon Band of Mission Indians	Bustamante, antirecall campaign	68
California Assn. of Highway Patrolmen	None	N/A
California Building Industry Assn.	None	N/A
California Democratic Party	antirecall campaigns	N/A
California Farm Bureau Federation	None	N/A
California Federation of Teachers	Bustamante, antirecall campaign	48
California Labor Federation	None	N/A
California/Nevada Conference of Operating Engineers	None	N/A
California Nurses Assn.	None	N/A
California Professional Firefighters	antirecall campaigns	N/A
California School Employees Assn.	Bustamante, antirecall campaign	29
California State Council of Laborers	Bustamante, antirecall campaign	47
California State Council of Service Employees	None	N/A
California State Pipe Trades Council	Bustamante, antirecall campaign	71
California Teachers Association	Bustamante, antirecall campaign	6

(continued)

Table 6.1 Continued

Donor	Recipient(s)	Days after recall certified that donor gave to Bustamante
California Union of Safety Employees	Bustamante, antirecall campaign	18
Genentech	Schwarzenegger, antirecall campaign	N/A
Goldenberg, Paul	Schwarzenegger, antirecall campaign	N/A
International Brotherhood of Electrical Workers	None	N/A
International Brotherhood of Teamsters	Bustamante, antirecall campaign	57
Laborers Union	None	N/A
L.A. County Service Employees	None	N/A
Mercury General Corp.	Schwarzenegger, McClintock, antirecall campaign	N/A
Operating Engineers Union	Bustamante, antirecall campaign	26
Orrick, Herrington, and Sutcliffe	Bustamante, antirecall campaign	54
Paramount Pictures	Schwarzenegger	N/A
Peace Officers Research Assn.	None	N/A
Plumbers and Pipefitters	Bustamante	54
Plumbers and Steamfitters	antirecall campaigns	N/A
Southern California Pipe Trades	None	N/A
Walt Disney	None	N/A

NOTE: Recall was certified on July 23, 2003.

that 14 donated to Schwarzenegger during the recall. That is, 54 percent of elite Republican donors gave to Schwarzenegger, while only 36 percent of elite Democratic donors gave to Bustamante.

This pattern is supportive of the picture painted by the interviews, suggesting that party pressure limited donor activity on Bustamante's behalf prior to September. These are the most active and loyal party donors, almost always contributing in party contests, and yet we see that fewer than half of them gave money to Bustamante. And just five of them (14 percent) gave money to Bustamante prior to September, even though he'd been running since July. This was how the party enforced its will; through the allocation of funds. These elite donors were the enforcers.

We can get another sense of the different donation patterns across party lines by examining the ideological range of donors for each candidate, which we can do thanks to Adam Bonica's (2013) Database on Ideology, Money in Politics, and Elections (DIME). Figure 6.3 shows a density plot of the ideological "ideal points" of people who donated to the candidates of the 2003 recall election, grouped by candidate. These ideal points are arrayed from –2 (the most liberal position) to +2 (the most conservative position). The peaks of each candidate distribution do a nice job showing the overall ideological positions of their supporters;

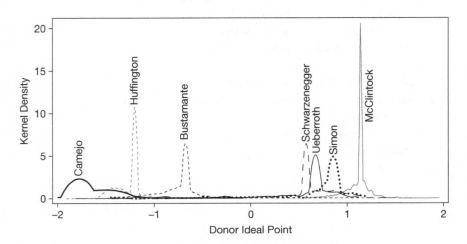

Figure 6.3 Ideal Points of Donors to Recall Race, by Candidate.
NOTE: Data come from the Database on Ideology, Money in Politics, and Elections (Bonica2013).

Table 6.2 MEDIANS AND STANDARD DEVIATIONS OF IDEAL POINTS OF RECALL
CANDIDATES' DONORS

Candidate	Median contributor ideal point	Standard deviation of contributor ideal points
Camejo (Green)	−1.748	0.251
Huffington (Independent)	−1.200	0.274
Bustamante (Democratic)	−0.673	0.290
Schwarzenegger (Republican)	0.572	0.409
Ueberroth (Republican)	0.671	0.515
Simon (Republican)	0.866	0.408
McClintock (Republican)	1.141	0.292

Bustamante and Schwarzenegger had the most moderate donor pools of their parties, McClintock's supporters were far to the right, and so on.

Also of interest, however, is the spread of these distributions. Table 6.2 shows the median and standard deviation of the ideal points of each candidate's donors. Notably, the standard deviation of Schwarzenegger's donors (.409) was substantially higher than that of Bustamante's donors (.290). This is more evidence that Schwarzenegger had a much more consolidated party behind him; the broad Republican coalition was overwhelmingly supporting him, while Bustamante had a hard time raising funds outside of his base.

Bustamante's difficulties in finding support for his campaign reflected the decision by Democratic leaders to maintain their united front in opposition to the recall and to any candidate entering as a replacement. Leaders hoped to pressure Bustamante out of the race, as they had with Garamendi and as Republicans had with several candidates. But Bustamante would not be driven out. As Bustamante consultant Richie Ross explained, there was a widespread stance that the lieutenant governor had "betrayed the establishment": "It was hard. He was a pariah. So was I."

The Democratic united front began to crack in late August when the state's congressional Democrats, the California Teachers Association, and a state firefighters union announced their endorsement of Bustamante, adopting his two-pronged slogan of "No on Recall, Yes on Bustamante" (LaVelle 2003). Four days later, the powerful California Federation of Labor reversed its position and announced its endorsement of Bustamante, as well (Sheppard 2003). Then on August 28, state party chair Art Torres announced that he would push to have the Democratic Party's executive council endorse Bustamante at its mid-September meeting (Kurtzman and Mintz 2003). This announcement was seen as tantamount to an endorsement itself.

Why did these Democratic leaders shift course suddenly? As consultant Richie Ross explains, their warning that the presence of a Democrat on the replacement ballot would make the recall more likely didn't seem to be panning out:

> There came a point where, okay, he's done it. Maybe he shouldn't have done it, or maybe I don't like that he's done it. But, hey, the contest is on, and there was never any poll that indicated that by entering the race he had done any damage to the yes or no question on the recall. So once people saw that . . . then this wasn't some giant act of betrayal as it played out. . . . People started saying, "What the hell? Why not give the guy some money just in case Gray doesn't make it?"

This combination of prominent officeholders, party officials, and labor union leaders changing their course and endorsing Bustamante as the party's favorite served as the de facto Democratic nomination of Bustamante. As Figure 6.4 demonstrates, Bustamante's fundraising success picked up

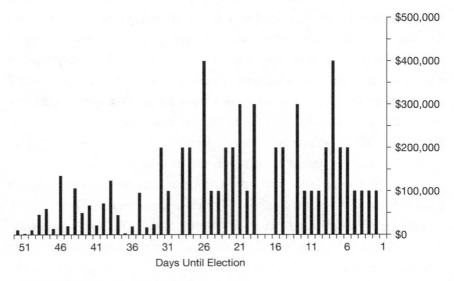

Figure 6.4 Bustamante Daily Fundraising Rate.

dramatically around 32 days out from the election—the beginning of September, right after these endorsements were made. His average daily fundraising rate tripled from $47,000 per day to $155,000 per day almost overnight.

The widespread party support for Bustamante helped transform the cartoonish recall race into a legitimate contest. Bustamante, Schwarzenegger, and McClintock (along with a few other candidates such as Arianna Huffington and Peter Camejo) participated in lively, substantive televised debates throughout late September. The party campaign machines kicked into gear and produced millions of dollars in advertising and voter persuasion literature.

In the end, the recall measure passed by a margin of 55 to 45, ending Gray Davis's two-decade career in California politics. Bustamante won only 31 percent of the vote—an impressive consolidation of liberal voters in a field of 135 candidates (including 47 other registered Democrats), but a somewhat paltry showing in a state that tends to lean strongly Democratic. He came in 18 points behind Schwarzenegger, who was sworn in as governor that November.

Democrats were obviously stung by the election results. This raised the question of what to do about Bustamante's major apostasy. According to reporter Dan Morain, "I think his entry into the race really, really damaged him." As Emerson describes it,

> I think some people got the message [about not entering the race]. Some people it sunk in a little slower, and then some people always think they're smarter, right? "Why should I listen to you? You've never done anything for me before." You know, and they get themselves trapped, and then guess what. Nothing's ever going to be done for you again.

According to Salazar, Bustamante became persona non grata among Democratic leaders across the state:

> He didn't get invited to a lot of the Democratic events, you know, where you showcase sort of your Democrats. There was nobody who actually went to him and said, "You're out," or anything to that effect.

But it was just that he stopped being able to raise money. . . . His funding sources dried up. A lot of the support from different groups and organizations dried up for him. You know, and that just made it extremely difficult, especially as he ran his insurance commissioner's race, for him to win beyond his base.

Whenever he would attend Democratic events, I don't think anybody ever said anything to him. . . . He wouldn't get the best speaking slots, and he'd be an afterthought in a lot of things. And I think that's the price he paid.

It should be noted that Bustamante still had enough of a faction of supporters and a financial base to prevail in the 2006 primary for state insurance commissioner. He won 70 percent of the vote against his one rival, John Kraft, a little-known heir to the Kraft Foods company, whose sole claim to fame was a role in the invention of individually wrapped American cheese slices and pourable salad dressing. A more structured and more vengeful party *could* have backed Kraft or recruited another candidate to run against Bustamante in the primary. Instead, state Democrats did little to aggressively hurt him, but did little to help him, either.

Even if Democratic leaders were angry at Bustamante, after all, they didn't necessarily blame him for the outcome of the recall election. Davis was truly unpopular and the recall seemed like it was going to pass regardless of whether the Democrats fielded a candidate. And the Schwarzenegger campaign struck many as a force of nature—an unusual blend of name recognition, media savvy, and timing that would have defeated even the strongest Democratic candidate at that time.

Bustamante went on to lose the general election in 2006, falling to Republican businessman Steve Poizner in a year that saw many Democratic gains throughout the country. It's certainly possible that a lack of support from Democratic allies undermined Bustamante's campaign. It's also possible that, as consultant Ross says, Bustamante's heart wasn't in it. For Ross, the whole recall experience was a fascinating wash: "I didn't make new friends, I didn't make new enemies."

DISCUSSION

To recall from the initial discussion above, the recall and replacement in California served as a powerful antiparty reform, even if that wasn't precisely their intent. Progressive reformers advocated them to help turn party hacks out of office and incentivize officeholders to demonstrate some distance from corrupt party bosses. And the unusual replacement mechanism, held simultaneously with the recall, having very low candidate entry thresholds, and involving no primary, caucus, or convention, seemed designed to undermine party organizations.

And yet as this chapter demonstrates, at the first serious statewide test of the recall (nearly a century after it went on the books), the parties proved more than able to surmount their considerable obstacles. In a field of 135 candidates, the parties managed to winnow the field such that many of the most serious candidates associated with either party either stayed out of the race or withdrew from it within a few weeks of filing. Republicans of a wide range of ideological stripes coordinated their efforts on electing Arnold Schwarzenegger and preventing a dilution of the Republican vote. They managed to convince many prominent, capable candidates, including a previous gubernatorial nominee and the one-time commissioner of Major League Baseball, to drop out and back their de facto nominee.

Democrats, meanwhile, converged on a strategy of not letting any candidate enter the replacement ballot, pressuring some very strong candidates to stay out. When Cruz Bustamante crossed that Rubicon, the opposition of labor groups and Democratic Party and elected officials hobbled his fundraising activities. The party ultimately relented and backed him, opening up much-needed funding for him to run a serious campaign, but it later ostracized him. His meteoric rise in California politics was shut down early due to his apostasy.

The institution of the primary election is highly cherished by parties, giving them the ability to coordinate their support on an unambiguous nominee. Yet as we have seen, even depriving them of this valuable institution doesn't necessarily undermine them. If a party cannot make an official nomination, then an unofficial nomination will do, as happened when the broader Republican and Democratic state party networks committed publicly for Schwarzenegger and Bustamante, respectively. No one paying attention to California politics in September of 2003 had any doubt of the parties' preferred candidates for the recall election.

The evidence provided in this chapter presents yet another example of a party adapting to and overcoming a reform expected to seriously harm it. Parties were simply not expected to be part of the recall and replacement, which were seen as ways to undermine them. As we have seen, the broader party networks can very much nominate candidates even in the absence of a primary; they simply do so in a less transparent way with less voter input.

7

Wisconsin's Adoption of the Direct Primary

The 20th-century drive for clean government, a public sector free of corrupt party bosses, and home to enlightened discourse among educated citizens really saw its genesis in the state of Wisconsin. In some ways the leader of the Progressive movement, Wisconsin was an early adopter of many key party reforms. Its status today as home to one of the nation's top public state university systems, most transparent and least corrupt state governments, and highest voter turnout rates stands as a testament to the institutions generated around the turn of the 20th century there.

The state is also a bit of a mystery. With political institutions designed to produce more moderate politicians, it nonetheless has a history of electing some of the more polarized and polarizing leaders the country has seen. Red-baiting conservative Senator Joe McCarthy, liberal Senator Russ Feingold (the only senator to oppose the USA-Patriot Act in 2001), and union-bashing governor Scott Walker all got elected by this moderate swing state.

But the state's political history makes for a useful test of the ideas presented in this book. Specifically, the state was the first to adopt the direct open primary in 1904.[1] Simultaneously praised as an attempt to

---

1. There is actually some debate over which state was the first to adopt the direct primary statewide. Depending on the precise definition of reforms, either Oregon, Minnesota, or Wisconsin is sometimes granted credit for coming first (Harvey and Mukherjee 2006).

drive corruption from government and decried as a move that would undermine party discipline, the open primary took the power of nomination away from bosses and conventions. Because it was a shock to the political system that occurred at a precise time in history, and because we have empirical measures of officeholder behavior at that time, we can examine a dramatic change in the system of party nominations on officeholders.

Quite simply, if any reform should influence officeholder behavior, it should be this one. Politicians who could be quickly made or broken by party bosses undoubtedly felt beholden to their masters. Conversely, politicians who had run for nomination in open primaries—at which all sorts of voters, even unaffiliated ones, could participate—likely felt beholden to a far more diffuse and less partisan constituency.

Yet as I show in this chapter, those predictions simply do not hold. Concerns about undisciplined parties proved unfounded, as not only did Wisconsin's legislative parties not decline, they actually strengthened under the direct primary. By several measures, the state's parties became more internally disciplined and ideologically more distant from each other, while legislators began representing their parties more than their constituencies. Consistent with other research, I find that party leaders are actually more capable of influencing primary election outcomes and controlling the behavior of primary-nominated politicians than is generally appreciated. This reform, designed to mitigate partisanship, may indeed have played a role in strengthening it.

In the next section, I examine predictions about the adoption of the direct primary and other reforms in the way candidates are nominated. I then look at the specifics of Wisconsin's embrace of this reform and the particular role played by Governor Robert La Follette in that struggle. I set up several testable hypotheses about the behavior of state legislators under the direct primary and then describe the evidence. I conclude by noting what the failure of the direct primary to moderate legislators means for our understanding of political parties and reform movements in general.

THE RISE OF THE DIRECT PRIMARY

The direct primary spread quickly and dramatically across the nation in the early 1900s. By 1915, 28 of the 37 nonsouthern states had adopted it (Lawrence, Donovan, and Bowler 2013). Although it had been employed at the municipal level in several areas previously—Milwaukee County, Minnesota, enacted such a law in 1891, for example, and Crawford County, Pennsylvania, began using primary elections as early as 1842—no state had attempted to impose such a nomination system statewide prior to 1900. In the vast majority of the 19th-century United States, candidates were nominated via party conventions, and those conventions were often dominated by a "boss" or small clique of insiders, who generally could produce the outcomes they wanted.

While the mechanism by which primaries were adopted is not in dispute, the motivations for it are, as I discussed in chapter 2. Scholarship investigating the transition from conventions to direct primaries is sharply divided over whether this was a revolution against party bosses or a clever adaptation by party leaders to preserve their power.

The former view has surely been the dominant one among political scientists and historians investigating the Progressive movement over the past century. In this framework, party bosses achieved their desired outcomes in politics largely by dominating the nomination of candidates; they could hand-pick candidates who would serve their interests and, because of their control over the machinery of politics, those candidates would remain faithful to them once in office. Hand-picking nominees was a relatively easy task in the world of the party convention, since bosses could control who participated in that convention. Beyond that, winning over a few hundred convention delegates was generally not difficult—people could be bought with promises, patronage jobs, or even outright bribes.

The direct primary was seen by reformers as a panacea to many of the nation's ills. It would restore political power to the people, free public officials from undue influence, and end the distorting influence of party on the political system (Smith and Azari 2015). As Reynolds (2006, 181–2) explains,

The direct primary was the special concern of a body of reforming professionals found in the newly nonpartisan (more accurately "bipartisan") urban press, in independent political organizations (like the National Municipal League), and in the academic community. A key motif of those who identified themselves as "progressives" was an appeal to the public interest. Their rhetoric was replete with references to "efficiency," "morality," "good government," and "the best men" who served the interests of all. They confronted political "bosses" who they claimed served only "selfish" interests.

In this view, the rise of the direct primary was a great threat to party bosses and fundamentally changed the character of party nominations. As Progressive reformers reasoned, "while it is not difficult to bribe or intimidate a few hundred convention delegates, it is impossible to suborn thousands of voters" (Ranney 1975, 124). They promised the direct primary would not only overthrow boss rule, but would result in more independent and better elected officials, an improvement in voter turnout due to citizen empowerment, and more accurate representation of the people's wishes (Ranney 1975). In other words, it was everything the party bosses feared. To them, the direct primary threatened to undermine party organization and destroy party discipline among officeholders (Philipp 1910). It would turn politics over to the rabble or, worse, leave them to the devices of the most articulate demagogue in any given election. The direct primary was, above all things, something to be feared and avoided by party machines.

A more recent view, however, casts some doubts on this interpretation. As Ware (2002) notes, it seems odd that party bosses, who allegedly controlled state legislatures and governors and regularly thwarted public opinion to achieve their desired policy ends, would lose on such an important matter in so many states at roughly the same time. How could they get everything they wanted except the one thing that mattered most to their continued control?

A more likely interpretation is that the direct primary, while certainly popular among the population, fulfilled a need for party bosses as well. That is, the primary brought in the state to settle party nomination disputes. Prior to the primary, a frustrated candidate denied the nomination in a party convention might work with allies to form a rival convention within the same party and claim that nomination. The lack of a final government arbiter in matters of nomination meant that it was sometimes unclear just who the nominee was, resulting in the dangerous situation of splitting the party and its vote. This was becoming more of a problem in the late 1800s as the numbers of candidates for office grew substantially, well ahead of the growth in the population, and it became more acceptable for candidates to display ambition rather than mask their desires under the cloak of party (Reynolds 2006). The direct primary solved this problem for all time.

The obvious downside of the primary, from the perspective of the party bosses, was that it really did empower voters to choose the party's nominee. This meant that party leaders now had to influence thousands of voters instead of hundreds of convention delegates. Again, though, this proved not to be onerous. With their outsized control of endorsements and campaign donations, party leaders could affect who the public would take seriously as a candidate. Indeed, party leaders continue to exert a powerful influence over primary voters in determining just who gets a party's nomination (Cohen et al. 2008; Dominguez 2005; Kousser et al. 2015; Masket 2009b).

We can also see reformers—those who advocated for the direct primary to dethrone the party bosses—as another form of party boss. After all, they did what any other would-be political leader might do, in that they sought a change in institutional rules that would favor their own leadership and disfavor someone else's (Trounstine 2008). Wisconsin's famous governor and senator Robert "Fighting Bob" La Follette provides an excellent example of just such an antiboss boss, as we will see in the next section.

LA FOLLETTE AND THE WISCONSIN IDEA

The state of Wisconsin political system was, at the turn of the 20th century, widely perceived to be under the dominion of the lumber and railroad industries (Lovejoy 1941). It was a perception common to many Progressive states, where extremely wealthy extraction and transportation companies tended to work in partnership with state political parties to control state politics and ensure that candidates and bills hostile to those industries never got elected or became law. As in many of those states, the Republican Party held large percentages of state legislative seats following the election of 1896, rendering Democrats largely inconsequential except when the Republican Party was split, which it soon would be.

Factionalism is certainly common among oversized legislative majorities, but the split that would occur within state Republican parties at the turn of the 20th century was unusually dramatic and continues to shape politics today. This split concerned Progressivism, a collection of policy prescriptions[2] for government, business, journalism, and nearly every other aspect of American public life. Chief among Progressives' political reform goals was the taming or even abolition of political parties, widely seen as corrupt entities preventing progress on matters important to the public. As the 1912 national Progressive platform declared in a section entitled "The Old Parties,"

> Behind the ostensible government sits enthroned an invisible government owing no allegiance and acknowledging no responsibility to the people. To destroy this invisible government, to dissolve the unholy alliance between corrupt business and corrupt politics is the first task of the statesmanship of the day. (Progressive Party 1912)

One of the most famous and articulate spokespeople for Progressivism was Wisconsin's Robert La Follette, a Madison attorney who served several terms in the US House of Representatives prior to his later statewide elections. Like many reformers within the Republican Party, he was bothered by the reputation of corruption his party had developed by the end of the 19th century. Teaming up with other reformers against the Stalwart Republicans, he sought his party's nomination for governor in 1896, running on a campaign of cleaning up politics and removing party bosses.

2. There is some scholarly debate over whether Progressivism should be considered an ideology distinct from liberalism or conservatism (Noel 2013).

When that campaign failed, he began to embrace the primary as the reform that would both clean up politics and clear the way for his own nomination. As Ware writes, La Follette "alighted on the direct primary as the means by which he and others could avoid being out-organized in the future" (Ware 2002, 126). La Follette railed against the party organizations in an 1897 address:

> This is the modern political machine. It is impersonal, irresponsible, extra-legal. The courts offer no redress for rights it violates, the wrongs it inflicts. It is without conscience and without remorse. It has come to be enthroned in American politics. It rules caucuses, names delegates, appoints committees, dominates the councils of the party, dictates nominations, makes platforms, dispenses patronage, directs state administrations, controls legislatures, stifles opposition, punishes independence, and elects United States senators. In the states where it is supreme, the edict of the machine is the only sound heard, and outside is easily mistaken for the voice of the people. (Lovejoy 1941, 36)

To the extent that La Follette accurately described party control, it was due in part to the complicated system of caucuses and conventions necessary to achieve the party's nomination in Wisconsin. "In years of presidential election," explains Lovejoy (1941, 17), "there were at least six caucuses in every voting precinct to determine the delegates to the various conventions." The only people with the skills and resources to master that system were party elites and industry leaders; a talented individual with a good set of policy ideas really didn't have much of a chance. At least in theory, such an individual might have a better chance if nominations were determined by a simple election. "Put aside the caucus and convention," La Follette implored Wisconsin. "They have been and will continue to be prostituted to the service of corrupt organization" (36). With the conventions gone, he promised, "no longer . . . will there stand between the voter and the [elected] official a political machine with a complicated system of caucuses and conventions,

by the easy manipulation of which it thwarts the will of the voter"
(Reynolds 2006, 184).

While direct primaries became popular in many other states in the first
decade of the 20th century, in few did the movement take hold quite as
quickly as in Wisconsin. La Follette's supporters and detractors both gave
him much of the credit for advancing the issue. According to Emanuel
Philipp, a stalwart Republican (who would later work for the railroad and
himself become governor), La Follette

> was wonderfully persuasive at times and his influence over some of
> his adherents had many of the characteristics of hypnotism. In no
> other way can be explained their consent to become involved in a
> political intrigue that would have been in place in a Latin American
> republic, but which was entirely foreign to Wisconsin methods.
> (Philipp 1910)

Philipp added that, according to La Follette,

> the stalwarts represented "special interests" as opposed to a great
> reform movement; that "organized greed" was arrayed to defeat the
> purposes of a highly virtuous and wholly unselfish band of patriots
> whose sole aim was to serve the people intelligently and faithfully. It
> was even asserted that the contest was between "the people" on one
> side and "the machine" on the other. (Philipp 1910)

By 1898, through its public persuasion campaign and a great deal of
organization in local caucuses, La Follette's Progressives had made some
inroads into the state GOP organization. The state's Democrats, meanwhile, actually fully endorsed direct primaries at their convention that
year. La Follette redoubled his efforts, putting the direct primary on
moral par with the liberation of slaves some decades earlier:

> To every generation some important work is committed. If this
> generation will destroy the political machine, will emancipate the
> majority from its enslavement, will again place the destinies of this

nation the hands of its citizens, then "Under God, this government of the people, by the people, and for the people shall not perish from the earth." (Unger 2000, 109)

By the time of the 1900 Republican convention, La Follette's Progressive team had managed to build up enough support at various caucuses to dominate the proceedings. Remarking on that convention, Judge E. W. Keyes, something of a Republican party boss in Wisconsin back in the 1870s, claimed that "a new cult has arisen and has forced its way to the front" (Lovejoy 1941, 53). La Follette was nominated for governor and won the contest handily that fall. He then quickly turned to the task of enacting his Progressive agenda, with the top items on his agenda being the direct primary and the regulation of railroad rates.[3] "Whoever seeks to thwart or defeat [direct nominations] is an enemy of representative government," La Follette threatened. "Let him beware!" (Unger 2000, 113) The bill's Stalwart detractors, meanwhile, described it as "radical to a Populistic degree" and "revolutionary in the worst sense of that word," and raised fears that it would destroy all party organization in Wisconsin (Unger 2000, 61).

La Follette's Progressive allies in the legislature introduced a direct primary bill early in the 1901 session. Its narrow passage in the House that March demonstrated the sharp splits within the state Republican Party during that era. Figure 7.1 charts the first and second dimension ideal points (estimates of legislator ideology based on their roll call voting behavior—more on this in the next section) for each member of the state Assembly in 1901. Each member is labeled both by his party ("D" or "R") and his vote on the primary bill (supporters are in uppercase letters, opponents are in lowercase). The dashed line marks the cut line (the best fit line for separating supporters and opponents) for the direct primary bill. As that line's placement suggests, the division on this vote essentially was the major cleavage in the chamber during that year. There was no major split between the parties; while Democrats are further to the "left"

3. La Follette's broader agenda included a laundry list of Progressive goals, including restrictions on lobbying and campaign expenditures, improvements to schools, smashing monopolies, and regulation of food, child labor, and the work environment (Unger 122).

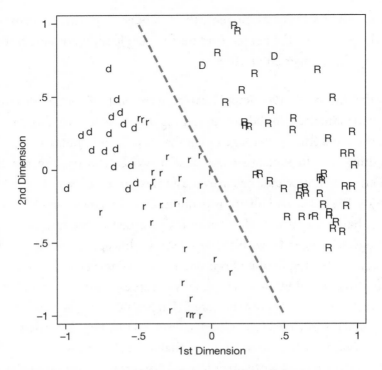

Figure 7.1 Ideal Points in 1901 House with Primary Vote Bill Cut Line.
NOTE: Each data point indicatesa member of the Wisconsin Assembly in 1901, mapped by his first and second dimension W-NOMINATE ideal point estimate. Data points are labeled by party and vote on Bill 98, a "bill to abolish political caucuses and conventions and provide for political nominations by direct vote," from 3/22/1901 (capital letters indicate supporters, lowercase letters indicate opponents).

than most Republicans,[4] there is substantial overlap between the parties. Rather, the main division was between Progressives and Stalwarts.

An analysis of the vote among Republicans suggests a strong ideological component. The analysis shown in Table 7.1 uses a Probit regression equation to predict the probability that a Republican House member voted in support of the primary bill. Several county-level indicators—the Democratic presidential vote share in 1900, the rural percentage,

---

4. I use the terms "left" and "right" very hesitantly and only in the most literal sense here. The W-NOMINATE calculation method simply scales members by ideal point and can't determine which members are ideologically left or right, and those terms are probably not appropriate for this era in US politics.

Table 7.1 PREDICTORS OF VOTE FOR DIRECT PRIMARY
IN WISCONSIN HOUSE AMONG REPUBLICANS

Variable	Model 1	Model 2
First-dimension ideal point		5.137***
		(1.209)
Democratic Presidential Vote, 1900	0.004	−0.063
	(0.037)	(0.095)
Percent Rural	−0.013	−0.016
	(0.012)	(0.034)
Percent German	−0.042	−0.063
	(0.060)	(0.133)
Percent Irish	−0.708*	−0.882
	(0.297)	(0.798)
Percent Scandinavian	0.021	−0.057
	(0.053)	(0.149)
Per capita income	−0.026	0.010
	(0.016)	(0.038)
Vote margin in 1900	0.000	−0.005
	(0.015)	(0.023)
Constant	2.868	4.455
	(2.200)	(5.990)
N	74	74
Pseudo-R^2	0.148	0.762

NOTE: Cell entries are Probit coefficients. Dependent variable
is the vote on the 3/22/1901 primary bill, with ayes coded one
and noes coded zero. Standard errors appear in parentheses.
Asterisks indicate statistical significance (* $p \leq .05$, ** $p \leq .01$,
*** $p \leq .001$).

several measures of foreign birth, and per capita income—are used as
independent variables, as is each legislator's winning vote margin in
the previous election. In the first model, only the Irish percentage of
the member's home county has a statistically significant relationship.
Perhaps unsurprisingly, those from more Irish counties are less sympathetic to Progressivism. But that relationship loses its statistical significance in the second model, which includes ideal points. A great deal

of the variance in the vote is explained by that variable alone. Notably, the pseudo R-squared increases from .15 to .73 when ideal points are inserted into the model.

What this analysis suggests is a substantial division within Wisconsin's Republican Party during this time period. Political reforms like the direct primary comprised the biggest set of issues the state government faced, and the majority party was deeply and ideologically split on it.

Despite its passage in the House, the primary bill soon met with obstacles in the Senate. It became quickly clear that there were insufficient votes to send a primary bill to Governor La Follette's desk. First-term Republican senator Henry Hagemeister of Green Bay introduced a compromise measure that would apply the direct primary only to local offices. The legislature passed this, and many Republicans urged La Follette to sign it, believing it was an important first step toward the Progressive's goal. La Follette, however, famously vetoed the bill, stating, "I believe in going forward a step at a time, but it must be a full step" (Unger 2000, 123–4).

La Follette and his supporters continued to press their case, even making his 1902 reelection campaign essentially a referendum on the direct primary. In 1903, the legislature passed and La Follette signed a statewide direct primary law; it was ratified by voters in a 1904 referendum, passing with 62 percent of the vote. The new law would go into effect in time for the 1906 election cycle.

PREDICTIONS, DATA, AND METHODS

Although Progressives and Stalwarts viewed politics in very different ways, their predictions associated with the direct primary are quite similar. Both expected that the direct primary would undermine, if not destroy, political parties. As Stalwart Emanuel Philipp summed up,

> Under [the direct primary's] influence and by reason of the opportunities it offers for personal politics, the work of party disintegration is going forward at an alarming pace and there is urgent need of some means by

which order may be brought out of the prevailing political chaos and
government by parties—real representative government—restored to
the people of the state. (Phillip 1910, 83)

He further suggested that Wisconsin's delegation to the US House of
Representatives was, as of 1910, being ignored by Republican leaders, in
large part because of the new law:

The Wisconsin members were ignored because they have ceased to
represent a party. There is no political party in Wisconsin today. Each
member represents an independent effort at the primary and the polls,
and he goes to Washington as an individual who has been elected on a
platform made by himself and presented to his constituents on the stump
or in the form of private campaign literature. The names "Republican"
and "Democrat" have no real meaning in Wisconsin today. Even the
members of Congress make their own platforms and stand on them,
there being no conventions of party representatives to perform that duty.
Each member of Congress is a party by himself, and he runs for office on
his own individual merits and the issues he may feel disposed to present
to the people and talk about. (Phillip 1910, 95–6)

La Follette and the Progressive reformers generally felt, similarly, that
the direct primary would weaken party organization and improve representation of the people's beliefs. Having politicians directly nominated by
voters, rather than by agents of party bosses, they reasoned, would free
legislators from needing to represent those partisan figures and would
allow them to vote their districts or their conscience.

The language used by Progressive and Stalwarts a century ago doesn't
precisely map into the political dialogue of today. While modern political journalists and reformers opine extensively about the dangers of
polarization, the main concern expressed back then was over boss control, a party system "owing no allegiance and acknowledging no responsibility to the people" (Progressive Party 1912). These aren't precisely the
same concepts, but they certainly rhyme. In either case, legislators are

widely perceived to be sticking too much to their party masters, and a reform is being sought to free them to vote their consciences or their districts.

If the predictions of these Progressives and Stalwarts were right, then we should observe two main effects of the direct primary on legislators' voting behavior. First, we would see a depolarization of the Wisconsin legislature after the implementation of the direct primary as legislators are freed from the party yoke. Second, we would observe legislators voting more in line with the preferences of their districts and less in concert with their fellow partisans. It is not clear just when we might see such a shift—it wasn't implemented until the 1906 election cycle, although legislators knew it was coming as early as 1903, and arguably earlier. But at some point in that first decade of the 20th century, we would see some evidence of depolarization and improved representation.

Depolarization can come in a variety of flavors, of course. Here, I examine two of them:

Hypothesis 1: The interparty distance in ideal points will decline after the implementation of the direct primary.

That is, there will be less distance between the two parties' median ideal points after 1905.

Hypothesis 2: The spread of ideal points within each party will be greater after the implementation of the direct primary.

That is, as party discipline theoretically declines, we would see the standard deviation of ideal points within each party increase, with members freer to vote in different ways than they were under boss rule.

The third prediction concerns representation, based on the claim that legislators elected under direct primaries would be freer of party constraints and could better represent their voters:

Hypothesis 3: Legislators will more closely adhere to their districts' preferences after the implementation of the direct primary.

To examine the behavior of Wisconsin legislators before and during the era of the direct primary, I extracted complete sets of roll call votes from journals of the Wisconsin Assembly between 1895 and 1911 (these were made available by HathiTrust Digital Library). Journals were downloaded as text documents, and a research assistant created an R script to extract roll call votes from each. These roll call votes were then converted into W-NOMINATE and DW-NOMINATE ideal points for each legislator in each year with the assistance of Keith Poole and the W-NOMINATE package for R (Poole et al. 2014). Ideal points range from −1 to +1, with more positive numbers tending to indicate more conservative voting behavior.[5]

RESULTS

Figure 7.2 shows the median ideal points by party and year for the Wisconsin Assembly. Contrary to expectations, there was no moderation after the implementation of the direct primary in 1906. Rather, Republican ideal points held largely steady throughout the time period. Democrats saw, on average, a sudden move to the center after 1901, but they moved back toward the extremes *after* the implementation of the direct primary. It's worth keeping in mind that Democrats were a small minority of the chamber during this time period, usually holding fewer than 20 of its 100 seats, meaning that its median ideal point may jump around a bit simply due to small sample size. Overall, however, the minimum distance between the parties occurred in 1905, but very shortly after the adoption of the direct primary, the parties repolarized to earlier levels. This evidence pretty sharply refutes Hypothesis 1.

---

5. The "liberal" and "conservative" designations do not easily apply to the years surrounding the turn of the 20th century. After all, while Progressives would certainly be considered liberal today on matters of business regulation, their views on race and voter turnout, for example, might be cast as conservative. Generally, Republicans in this period had higher scores and Democrats had lower ones.

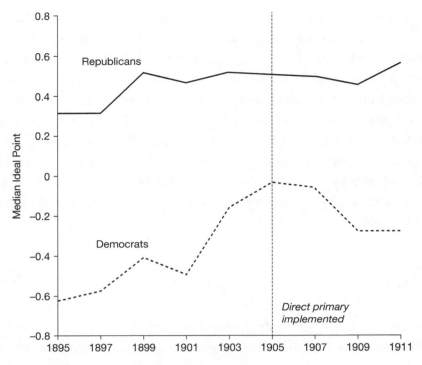

Figure 7.2 Ideal Points in the Wisconsin Assembly by Party.

To get a better sense of how internally heterogeneous the parties became, Figure 7.3 presents the standard deviations of ideal points within the parties. The line for the Democrats bounces around a good deal, again a function of the small sample size. The majority Republicans, however, see their standard deviation drop around the time the direct primary is implemented, suggesting the party actually became *more* internally coherent and disciplined. Indeed, the standard deviation among Republicans actually drops despite the fact that the number of Republicans in the chamber increases to its highest point in this time series by 1911. The GOP was, in a real sense, a stronger party under the direct primary.

I next turn to the analysis of representation in the Wisconsin Assembly. Precisely measuring the degree to which a legislator is representing her district is a difficult task even when data are plentiful, which they are not in this case. Recent studies that manage to ask legislators and voters the same question or otherwise place them on the same scale are perhaps the gold

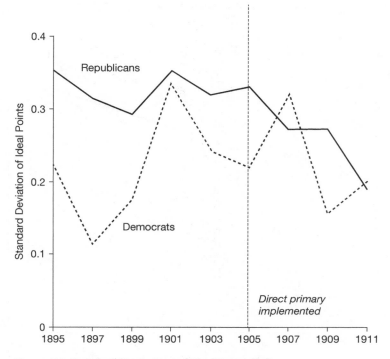

Figure 7.3 Standard Deviations of Ideal Points by Party.

standard (Bafumi and Herron 2010; Masket and Noel 2012), but turn-of-the-20th-century Wisconsin falls well short of that. One problem is that even if we have a measure of constituency's preferences (such as its vote in a presidential election), that is not necessarily on the same scale as a legislator's roll call ideal point. The most conservative legislator could be much more conservative, or more liberal, than the most conservative district. There is the additional problem that, at least in this case, presidential votes are aggregated at the county level rather than the legislative district level. Some legislative districts contain multiple counties, while some counties contain many districts. (In 1901, Milwaukee County contained 15 state assembly districts.)

Nonetheless, we can at least get a rough idea about the representational relationship between legislators and constituencies by comparing county-level presidential votes with assembly members' ideal points. With the aforementioned caveats in mind, we can examine Figure 7.4, which compares county-level presidential votes in 1900 with the legislators' ideal

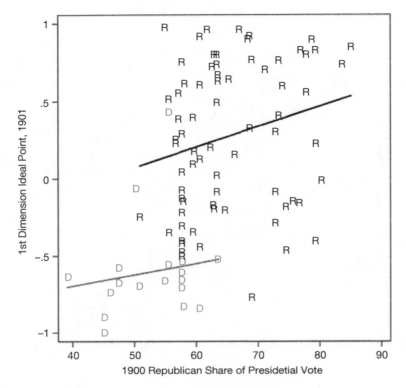

Figure 7.4 Representation in the 1901 Wisconsin Assembly.
NOTE: Each data point represents an Assembly member, mapped by the Republican share of the two-party presidential vote in their home county in 1900 and their first dimension W-NOMINATE ideal point in 1901.Trend lines are shown for each party.

points in 1901. Both axes are scaled in the Republican direction. If constituents are being represented, we would expect to see more Republican counties being served by legislators with more consistently Republican voting behavior. As the figure shows, there is some party-level and individual-level representation occurring in 1901. Republicans do represent more Republican counties than Democrats do, unsurprisingly, but even within each party, more Republican-leaning districts are represented by more Republican-leaning legislators. Both party trend lines slope upwards.

This makes an interesting contrast with Figure 7.5, which charts county-level presidential votes in 1908 against legislators' ideal points in 1911. While Republicans represent more Republican constituencies than Democrats do,

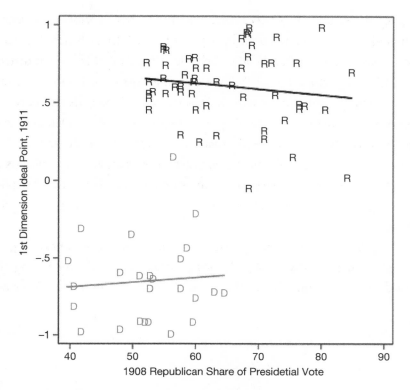

Figure 7.5 Representation in the 1911 Wisconsin Assembly.
NOTE: Each data point represents an Assembly member, mapped by the Republican share of the two-party presidential vote in their home county in 1908 and their first dimension W-NOMINATE ideal point in 1911.Trend lines are shown for each party.

within the parties there is functionally no representational relationship at all. A Republican representing a very competitive county votes no more or less with his party than one representing a county that voted overwhelmingly for Taft in 1908. This is evidence of considerable party discipline in 1911; legislators are voting their party and largely ignoring their constituents.

This is essentially the opposite of what Progressives had promised and anticipated. Politicians were supposed to be freer of party obligations and incentivized to represent their constituents. Instead we see highly disciplined parties largely insensitive to voters.

We can further examine this by systematically examining the relationships between district sentiments and legislator behavior over time. For each legislative session between 1903 and 1911, I have performed a regression analysis using the Republican share of the vote in each state legislative district election to predict the ideal point for the member from that district. Legislative district elections aren't perfect indicators of district sentiment—incumbents can sometimes win by larger margins than district partisanship would predict—but they give us a rough idea of how Democratic or Republican a district is. I have eliminated districts with uncontested elections from this analysis. The R-squared for each regression analysis gives us an idea of how well district partisan leanings predict member voting behavior. The R-squareds for Democrats, Republicans, and all members are charted in Figure 7.6.

As the figure demonstrates, district voting behavior was never a good predictor for legislative roll call voting among Republicans during this period. Among Democrats, it began with modest predictive power and

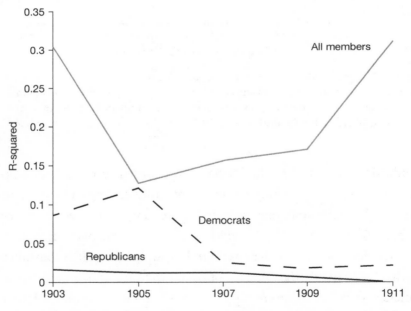

Figure 7.6 R-squared Analysis of District Votes Predicting Roll Call Votes.
NOTE: The points above are the R-squareds resulting from regressing 1st dimension DW-NOMINATE ideal points on the Republican share of the two-party vote in each member's district in the previous election. Districts with uncontested legislative races are not included in the analysis.

then bottomed out under the direct primary. The pattern among all members vacillates substantially, but by the end of the time series it's no stronger than it was at the beginning. Overall, members don't seem to be voting their districts any better under the direct primary, and by some measures they're doing a worse job. Members seem to be sticking with their parties more than with their districts.

Why would this happen? Even if the direct primary didn't obliterate Wisconsin's parties, shouldn't it have damaged them somewhat, even temporarily? It was, if nothing else, a shock to the system. Why did partisanship not only not decline, but actually increase by some measures?

To be sure, we have plenty of evidence in the decades since the broad adoption of the direct primary that party leaders are just as capable at managing outcomes of primaries as those of conventions. Through strategic disbursements of endorsements, money, and campaign expertise, party leaders can signal to interest groups, activists, and voters which candidates are appropriate for the party and which are not, and they rarely end up with election outcomes they did not plan. But this adaptation no doubt took time. In Wisconsin, why do we see no temporary dip in polarization with the rise of the new reform?

The evidence here is somewhat more tentative, but it appears that some of the fears of the Stalwarts were well founded. The direct primary didn't create chaos; rather, it allowed for the rise of new bosses to replace the old ones. La Follette himself was, by no small measure, a strong party leader. Even after his major reform had passed, he continued to exert great influence over the Republican Party, sometimes intimidating people into supporting him and his various crusades. In the words of Wiebe (1967, 215), La Follette "commanded respect without kindling affection." According to Ranney (1975, 26), he created a "reform machine": "He dexterously used patronage appointments, stump oratory, legislative logrolling, and any other method that seemed useful to convert or defeat his political opponents."

One of the best examples of this was the 1904 state Republican convention, held at the gymnasium at the University of Wisconsin's Madison campus. One of the key tasks of this convention was to select delegates to the national Republican convention that year, and Progressives wanted to make sure that those who held their beliefs represented those views to the national party. La Follette resorted to boss-like tactics to make sure his supporters ended up as national delegates:

> To eliminate the opposition in this mid-May convention, La Follette ordered the construction of a barbed-wire passage to force the delegates to enter the red brick gymnasium of the University of Wisconsin at Madison single file. He manned that passage with menacing guards (primarily university athletes). La Follette claimed such measures were necessary to prevent the convention from being taken unfairly and by force. (Unger 2000, 133)

Stalwarts protested and eventually bolted to a nearby opera house to form their own convention and slate of delegates. The Republican national credentials committee initially chose to seat the Stalwart delegates. However, after La Follette's direct appeal to President Theodore Roosevelt, and a ruling by the state Supreme Court and secretary of state, the Progressive delegation was ultimately seated.

DISCUSSION

The example of Wisconsin provides important evidence about the nature and consequences of party reform efforts. After all, the adoption of the direct primary is one of the most consequential reforms to the system of party nominations ever seen in the United States, and it is a system that still stands the United States apart from many other mature democracies around the world. Surely a shift of that magnitude should undermine parties.

Yet the history presented here offers another example of the tendency of reforms aimed at undermining parties to fail. For one thing, as we have seen, parties are highly adaptive; the direct primary did not take party leaders out of the role of selecting nominees, it simply changed the

means by which they did so. Party leaders were able to guide voter preferences and determine the outcome of primary elections just as surely as
they determined the outcome of party caucuses and conventions. What's
more, elected officials knew this, and they didn't stray far from what their
leaders wanted from them.

Second, as the Wisconsin example makes abundantly clear, reformers
themselves may serve as bosses. In this case, a faction of the Republican
Party that found itself on the losing end of many intraparty battles championed a reform that make their candidates' nominations more likely. An
open primary contest, with mass speeches and debates instead of deal
making inside convention halls, was a perfect venue for a fiery orator like
La Follette. As described in chapter 2, reform may just be a name we apply
to the party machine that opposed the previous party machine.

This is not to say that the direct primary had no effect. Much as
Stalwarts feared, it increased the costs of campaigns substantially (Philipp
1910). Parties and candidates now had to spend a great more time on the
campaign trail, paving the path to the near-constant campaign we see
in modern American politics. But this, too, would be a change to which
parties could adapt.

8

Quit Fixing It

You're Only Making It Worse

The previous chapters have delineated a series of attempts by state policymakers to rein in or eliminate political parties. The attempts vary a great deal in terms of the methods used, the precise problem being targeted, the place and time of the attempt, and so forth. But one thing that they all have in common is failure. Campaign finance restrictions failed to keep Colorado's Democratic Party from funding its preferred candidates. The direct primary failed to elect politicians who were more independent of their parties. Nonpartisan elections ultimately failed to prevent polarization in Minnesota and Nebraska.

And yet a reformer may legitimately look at these examples and draw motivation, rather than discouragement. After all, it's not as though these reforms had no effect at all; Minnesota and Nebraska really did see less polarized politics, at least for a while. And if the only reason reforms fail is because party actors respond rationally to them, well perhaps that just means that reforms need to come more often, keeping parties from successfully adapting. Besides, even if a reform is doomed to fail, what's the harm in trying? Perhaps each attempted reform gets us one step closer to the one that will finally succeed in driving partisanship from our politics.

These arguments, while certainly valid, overlook one key point: reforms are not costless exercises. Each attempt to drive parties from the political sphere exacts a price on democracy, decreasing transparency, accountability, and other things we claim to hold important in our governing systems. This chapter is an attempt to detail some of the costs of reforms. I divide the chapter into two main pieces, one on campaign finance reform, and the other on the role that parties tend to play in a representative government and what happens when no one is there to fill that role.

THE PRICE OF CAMPAIGN FINANCE REFORM

Campaign finance reform deserves its own section in this chapter because it is an area that goes well beyond party reform. Changing the way our campaigns are financed has become a business unto itself, an ongoing crusade to rid politics of the scourge of money and, indeed, corruption. For such reformers, money is an inherent evil in politics. Money, to them, buys influence, and thus those with more money have more influence and can bend government to their will.

One campaign finance reform advocacy group called Get Money Out advertised in 2011, "Bailouts. War. Unemployment. Our government is bought, and we're angry." The implication here is that somehow bailouts, war, and high unemployment are the results of private campaign spending. This, of course, is belied by the fact that nations with little or no private spending in campaigns (much of Europe, for example) have still struggled with high unemployment and finance sector bailouts in recent years, and it's not terribly obvious which moneyed interests are advocating war and unemployment. The group Get Money Out is hardly representative of all advocates of campaign finance reform, but it is emblematic of a tendency to view all of society's ills as resulting from wealthy interests steering government away from the public's interests and toward their own.

It should be noted here that political scientists have generally had a very difficult time identifying any effect of campaign spending on the behavior of elected officials. To be sure, there are occasional examples of outright corruption—Representative Duke Cunningham (R-CA) accepting a yacht in exchange for preferential treatment of a defense contractor, Governor Rod Blagojevich (D-IL) selling a US Senate seat, and so on—but such examples are extremely rare and, notably, already illegal and punishable by prison time. The more typical transactions of campaign money generally do not seem to actually induce any changes in politician's behavior. Indeed, the consensus finding is that money follows votes, instead of the reverse; donors give to candidates to reward desirable behavior rather than to induce it.

But what effects have we seen from various efforts to restrict campaign donations in the United States? For one thing, not only aren't these laws mitigating partisanship, they're actually intensifying it. As La Raja and Schaffner (2015) find, states with rules limiting the ability of parties to directly fund candidates have seen more rapid polarization than other states. The reason, they argue, is that formal party organizations tend to fund more moderate candidates, usually those in competitive elections. With such funding sources limited, the remaining donors to races—individuals, interest groups, unions, and so on—tend to be more ideologically motivated and to back a more extreme set of candidates.

Another notable effect is that donations have become much harder to track. One of the basic and broadly supported principles motivating campaign finance law is that of transparency. Political leaders have strong disagreements over whether campaign donations or expenditures should be limited and by how much, but there is a widespread consensus that donations should be recorded and that this information should be available to the general public as quickly as possible. Few are under the impression that voters will sit down at a computer on the eve of an election to review campaign finance disclosures and decide which candidate's supporters are more wholesome. But following a firefighting model of oversight, voters will rely upon reporters, watchdog activists, and rival campaigns to find donations that may appear to involve conflicts of interest. If a candidate advocating increased use of hydraulic fracturing for energy production is receiving millions of dollars from natural gas companies, it is presumably in the public's interest to know this. Furthermore, candidates, knowing that receiving funds from unsavory sources will eventually become news, will tend to avoid soliciting such support.

For decades, the federal government and most state governments have thus required that all donations to candidates above some modest threshold be recorded and made public. The federal government actually established such reporting requirements with the Tillman Act of 1907, but these disclosures were rarely enforced with much efficacy until the passage of the Federal Election Campaign Act in 1971. Most states have followed suit in the ensuring years.

Such disclosures are useful when the typical donation goes from an identifiable donor to an identifiable candidate. However, following the money becomes immeasurably harder when intermediaries are involved. Under such legislation as Colorado's Amendment 27, which I discussed in chapter 3, that's precisely what happened.

Amendment 27 was roughly a state-level analog to the national Bipartisan Campaign Reform Act (BCRA) of 2002, also known as McCain-Feingold. Amendment 27, approved by two-thirds of Colorado's voters in 2002, established limits on what individuals and parties could donate to state candidates; no limits on party donations to candidates had existed previously. The amendment barred corporations and unions from donating to parties, and it lowered individual donations to parties from $25,000 to $3000 (Fish 2002). The goal was to "reduce the impact special interests have on the political process and increase the influence of individual citizens" (Bender 2002). It was widely expected to have a devastating impact on the state's parties: "The reduction in donations would mean at least $4.7 million less for the state's Democratic Party this year and almost $1 million [less] for the Republican Party, which is receiving the bulk of its funds from the national GOP" (Fish 2002). According to Democratic Party chairman Tim Knaus, "It means the end of parties as they currently exist. I don't know what the new party looks like, but I can tell you that we will not be able to pay the lease" (Ames 2002). Knaus expected he'd have to fire all but one employee under the new rules.

There was a loophole, however, embedded within section 527 of the US Tax Code. Individuals could donate to new independent campaign organizations (dubbed 527s), which could in turn spend unlimited amounts of money on behalf of candidates, so long as they did not explicitly advocate the election or defeat of a candidate. The reform legislation could not change the fact that there were hundreds or thousands of individuals wishing to spend money to attempt to influence an election and plenty of candidates eager to receive it. All it could do was interrupt one conduit for that transaction.

How does a watchdog organization or journalist now track campaign money? Well, it's *possible* to examine the campaign disclosure records of a 527 organization to see who donated to it and how much they gave. But where did that money end up? Since a 527 can't coordinate directly with a candidate, it generally spends its money in a more dispersed manner. If it wants to boost voter turnout to help a particular campaign, it might hire a local campaign firm that specializes in voter turnout efforts, or it might hire a direct-mail consultant to target several neighborhoods with turnout messages, or it might pay local radio or television stations to run advertisements. The 527 is supposed to report in its filings just which candidates are benefiting from these expenditures, but that's not terribly precise. If you're reminding voters to turn out for Hillary Clinton in 2016, after all, you're probably also encouraging them to vote for Democratic candidates for Congress and state legislature, too, even if you don't mention it explicitly. So figuring out which campaign benefited from the money isn't easy or obvious.

But it gets more complicated than that. One of the advantages that Colorado's innovative Gang of Four had was that it often caught Republican candidates off guard. Few expected to see so much funding coming out of 527s in the 2004 election cycle. The Democrats maintained this imbalance by dismantling those 527s and creating new ones with different names for 2006. They did the same in subsequent elections, making it difficult for journalists or Republican strategists to know just where the next barrage of funds was coming from. What's more, they were coordinating all these donations across a vast web of liberal interest groups, labor unions, 527s, political action committees, independent expenditure groups, official party organizations, and individual donors. By 2010, the liberal umbrella organization AmericaVotes was coordinating spending across 37 different organizations. A diagram of these byzantine spending channels can be seen in Figure 8.1. A 2012 *Denver Post* profile of this network revealed some of the laborious work necessary to follow the money under such a campaign finance regime. Some of the records they sought were available electronically, but independent expenditure committees make only hard copies available, which had to be obtained from the secretary of state's office (Crummy 2012). Karen Crummy, the author of the piece, estimates she spent roughly 100 hours examining these disclosures in order to map out the network.

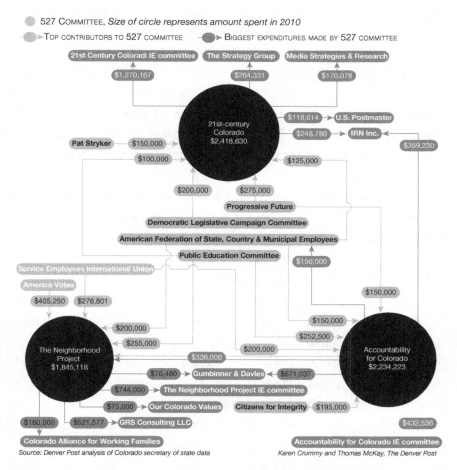

Figure 8.1 Depiction of Campaign Finance in 2010 Colorado Democratic State House Campaigns and Affiliated 527s.
SOURCE: Denver Post (Crummy 2012)

Needless to say, this complexity runs strongly against the principle of transparency, and it makes a mockery of disclosure requirements. But campaign finance limits only incentivize this sort of activity. If you want a candidate to win, it makes far more sense to finance that candidate by means of 527s and Super PACs—with unlimited spending capabilities and spotty disclosure requirements—than via limited direct donations.

The situation is arguably worse thanks to the rise of 501(c)(4) charitable organizations in politics. These groups are treated as nonprofits under the law as long as less than half of their funds are used toward electioneering, meaning that they are under no obligation to publicize their donors' names. Karl Rove's Crossroads GPS is one such organization. It spent more than $70 million in the 2012 cycle with no real disclosure requirements. Many object to the lack of transparency there, but what about disclosing the names of those who donate to the 501(c)(4) run by the League of Conservation Voters? Many of those donors may legitimately give with the expectation that their money will be used only for the social welfare functions of the group, such as raising awareness of environmental issues, and not on electioneering. Should their contributions be disclosed? It's possible that these groups provide legitimate public goods, but some donors would be less inclined to support them if it resulted in their name going onto a state or federal website. Yet this mix of charitable and more explicitly political work by 501(c)(4)s makes following the money all the harder.

Figure 8.2 demonstrates the growth of these alternative funding mechanisms over time. It shows two trends from 1998 to 2012. The first (the trendline) is the total spending on federal campaigns, including congressional and presidential. These spending figures include not just spending by the official campaign committees, but also "outside" spending, including that by 527s, PACs, party committees, independent expenditure groups, and others. While there are clear spikes in presidential years, the overall trend has been steadily upward, with spending increasing an average of 35 percent per election cycle, more than ten times the monetary inflation rate. Spending on the 2012 elections ($6.3 billion) was roughly double what it was in 2000 ($3.1 billion).

The second trend is marked by bars, showing the percentage of all this spending that was "outside" money. By its nature, outside money is more

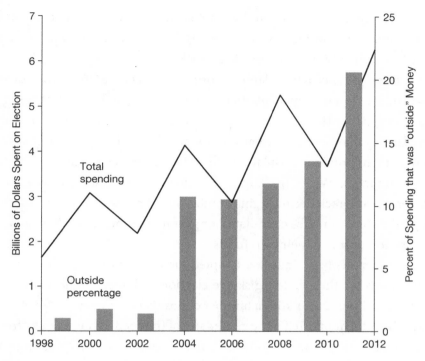

Figure 8.2 Spending and Outside Money in Federal Elections, 1998–2012.
SOURCE: OpenSecrets.org

difficult to trace. As described above, it is more challenging to figure out where the funds originated and track them to where they ended up, and it can be difficult to know just which election they were intended to influence. The outside percentage has jumped sharply at two times. The first, and largest, jump came in 2004, when the percentage shot up from 1 to 11 percent of spending. This was in response to BCRA, which had recently banned much direct spending by parties and their ability to raise "soft money." Cut off from this source of funds, party actors responded by helping to develop 527s, dramatically increasing the proportion of federal funds that were difficult to trace. The other major jump in outside spending came in 2012, following the US Supreme Court's 2010 decision in *Citizens United* v. *Federal Elections Commission*. As this decision relaxed some of BCRA's restrictions on campaign expenditures by corporations, unions, 527s, Super PACs, and other entities, it is not surprising that it appears to have coincided with a rise in the outside spending percentage.

The result of all this is that in the 2012 election cycle, more than one dollar in five spent on federal campaigning came through an outside path and was difficult if not impossible to track.

Is there an alternative? Some reformers, concerned about the corrosive influence of money on politicians, have proposed floors on campaign spending rather than ceilings. That is, instead of creating limits on what candidates may spend or what donors may have, they propose that the government provide candidates with sufficient money to run a competitive campaign. While the Supreme Court's interpretation of the First Amendment precludes outright prohibitions of private campaign spending,[1] the state can offer candidates ample public funds in exchange for a pledge to not spend their own funds.

Several states have, in fact, attempted such publicly funded, or "clean," campaigns for their state legislative elections: Maine, Connecticut, and Arizona. Miller (2013) finds a number of positive outcomes related to this experiment. For one, relieving candidates of the need to raise money frees up a great deal of campaign time. Candidates report using this time to walk precincts and meet with voters, theoretically placing them in greater contact with a wider range of their constituency than fundraising would. This has the effect of boosting voter participation in these down-ballot elections. Removing private funding from elections does not appear to moderate candidates, but it may have some other positive externalities. The lessons are not yet fully clear from a few states' relatively brief experiment with public funding (Hall 2014; Masket and Miller 2015). Nonetheless, it remains an option for those who see fundraising as an inherent conflict of interest for political candidates.

THE PRICE OF NONPARTISANSHIP

As discussed in the first two chapters of this book, much of the public finds political parties deeply frustrating entities. Indeed, a recent survey

---

1. *Buckley v. Valeo*, 424 U.S. 1 (1976).

found that Americans see political parties as our most corrupt governing institution, with three-quarters of all respondents labeling them as corrupt (Transparency International 2013). Now, it's hard to know just what respondents meant by "corrupt" when responding to that question—they probably don't mean that the parties are behaving dishonestly in exchange for money—but it seems fair to take this as evidence that the public simply finds the parties loathsome.

This is hardly a novel finding, and it is hardly unique to the United States. Indeed, in the survey above, respondents in two-thirds of the countries being studied labeled political parties as the most corrupt public institution. But it serves as a reminder that those political actors who wish to reform politics even for particularly self-serving ends can usually find willing allies in the American people if they frame their reform as curbing the power of parties.

It is to the point where parties are a convenient kick-dog in political debates, beloved roughly as much as terrorists and collections agencies. Witness the 2012 campaign over California's Proposition 14, the top-two proposal referenced in the introduction. Proponents of the initiative focused on the evils of parties and how their plan would curb some of those evils. As the pro-ballot argument averred,

Non-partisan measures like Proposition 14 will result in elected representatives in Sacramento and Washington who are LESS PARTISAN and MORE PRACTICAL. (California Secretary of State 2010; emphasis in original)

Did opponents defend parties? No. Rather, the con arguments in the ballot simply accused the backers of the initiative of misrepresenting their case and really just seeking to boost the careers of a handful of politicians. It is most telling that opponents of one of the most baldly antiparty proposals of recent years would not include a defense of parties in their arguments.

This is certainly understandable in terms of political realities. After all, while there are very good reasons for treating convicted murderers humanely, few politicians will make those arguments publicly. But it is nonetheless regrettable in terms of civic understanding. Parties are profoundly useful and beneficial for our democracy, and efforts to weaken them actually undermine many of democracy's virtues.

Take, for example, the composition of the electorate. In recent years, we have seen something of a bifurcation of goals with regard to voter turnout. Liberals and conservatives alike seem to prefer a large and informed electorate, but liberals are increasingly emphasizing the *large* part, advocating easier access to the ballot and raising sharp objections when a proposal arises to restrict access to the polls with voter identification laws. Conservatives, meanwhile, are placing increasing value on the *informed* part of the electorate. See, for example, this editorial from the right-leaning *Colorado Springs Gazette* (2008):

> People who don't vote play a positive role by not polluting election results with ill-informed decisions. . . . Ill-informed voters . . . do themselves and their country a giant favor by respectfully declining to vote. It requires no apology, no explanation. It's the noble, righteous and patriotic choice.

It seems fair to say, though, that if a large and informed (and legal) electorate showed up for an election, that would be treated as an unequivocal positive by all sides. But here's the rub: removing parties from the equation undermines both values. As mentioned in chapter 5, several researchers compared Minnesota state senate elections between 1972 (when the state still had a nonpartisan ballot) and 1976 (after the state's switch to a partisan ballot) (Schaffner, Streb, and Wright 2001). One of the things they found is that ballot rolloff decreased between those two elections. That is, people who showed up to vote for the presidential or congressional races were more likely to cast a vote in the state legislative races when the latter were partisan. They also found that incumbency had less of an effect on the vote when the partisan ballot was restored. Incumbents still tended to do better than challengers, but not by as much when voters could see the partisan identity of the candidates.

Why did these changes occur? The simple answer is that most voters have very little sense of who their state legislative candidates are. Surveys suggest roughly half as many citizens can name their state legislator as can name their member of Congress (Jewell 1982), and only a minority of voters even know which party holds the majority in their state legislature (Rogers 2013). State legislative candidates rarely have large advertising budgets and are usually dependent upon candidates further up the ballot for voter turnout efforts. The typical state legislative race cost just over $80,000 in 2010, compared to $2.5 million for the average US House race that year. Relatedly, there is little media coverage of state legislative activity when compared to congressional or presidential actions. Political postures and trial balloons by members of Congress can usually earn front-page coverage and invitations to appear on talk shows, and presidents can appear on the front of a newspaper just for going on a vacation. State legislators, however, work in comparative anonymity, and newspaper coverage of state capitols has been on the decline for decades. As a result, it is no wonder that state legislative races so closely mirror national trends (Rogers 2013).

There is thus a vast information gap for most Americans' understanding of state legislative elections. Parties are the greatest tool we've devised to help fill that gap. While most voters may not know the names of their legislators or even be able to recognize them on the street, they do understand the "D" or "R" that appears next to their name on the ballot. That single letter carries a tremendous amount of information with it. Simply by knowing a candidate's party affiliation, a voter has a very high probability of knowing that candidate's stances on abortion, gun laws, health reform, tax rates, union power, affirmative action, and dozens of other issues.

This was not always so. In the mid-20th century, America's political parties were famously diverse. The parties contained liberals, moderates, and conservatives. The Democratic caucus of the 88th US Senate (1963–64) included both Minnesota civil rights advocate Hubert Humphrey (with a DW-NOMINATE ideal point of –.377) and South Carolina segregationist Strom Thurmond (with an ideal point of .652). George Wallace's 1968 lament that there wasn't "a dime's worth of difference" between the two

major parties wasn't far from the mark. Over the past half-century, however, the parties have notably polarized. They have become more internally
coherent, with moderates steadily being purged through primary challenges (Boatright 2013), and they have become more distinct from each
other in the process.

Like many aspects of parties, this polarization has been widely
lamented. Pundits, politicians, and others routinely complain that the parties are talking past each other and that the kinds of compromises that
were possible back when Speaker O'Neill and President Reagan could just
get together for a stiff drink just don't exist anymore. The source of this
polarization is often—and inaccurately—attributed to personal or cultural
features (politicians travel too much, they don't sleep enough, they don't
get to know each other, the partisan media makes them say bad things,
the president hasn't set an adult tone, etc.). Party polarization, in fact, is
determined by powerful historical forces and is more properly considered
the norm (Ansolabehere, Snyder, and Stewart 2001), with the 1950s–1980s
the anomalous period in American political history. As Matthew Yglesias
(2009) writes, "I think polarization is a good thing but even if you disagree
the only proven way to minimize it is to have a large and influential white
supremacist movement obtain substantial congressional representation."

But regardless of the provenance of polarization, it is in fact a great
opportunity for voters rather than a source of woe. Parties are, to repeat,
voters' primary means of understanding the ballot, and that party label is
of value only to the extent that the parties are different from each other.
That is to say, party polarization makes elections more meaningful.
While voters may have little idea who runs what in a state legislature or
in Congress, they do have some sense of the direction the government is
heading, and they can decide whether to reward the governing party by
voting for it or punish it by turning its members out. Fifty years ago, a
dissatisfied electorate could cast an angry vote and toss many incumbents
out, but still end up with roughly the same policies coming out of that
government. Today, voting the majority party out of office will result in
very different policies.

This logic has become especially relevant at the level of state politics in
recent years. As of 2015, 41 states had both legislative chambers under the

control of the same party, down slightly from the record postwar high of 43 after the 2012 elections. Additionally, the nation is currently experiencing some of the highest numbers of unified party control states (with the governor and legislature under the same party) in the modern era (National Conference of State Legislatures 2015). And this is occurring at a time when the parties, nationally and in most states, are moving apart from each other and becoming more ideologically coherent (Shor and McCarty 2013). Voters, at least at the state level, are increasingly picking unified, programmatic party government.

The results, in terms of public policy, are both predictable and profound. While the national legislature is mired in acrimony and gridlock, state legislatures are legislating at dizzying paces, and marching away from each other in the process. While Wisconsin's Republicans gut public employee unions, Colorado's Democrats are passing handgun restrictions. Texas's Republicans were shuttering abortion clinics while Minnesota's DFLers were permitting same-sex marriage. Arizona's Republicans can crack down on illegal immigrants just as quickly as California's Democrats can pass new environmental regulations. Where we choose to live and how we decide to vote have greater relevance to our lives than at any other point in modern history (Masket 2013b).

This is precisely the point at which we need parties to structure our votes. As Schattschneider (1942, 52) wrote, "The people are a sovereign whose vocabulary is limited to two words, 'Yes' and 'No.' This sovereign, moreover, can only speak when spoken to." When state governments are radically experimenting with laws that determine whether the police may indiscriminately inspect us, whether we can easily vote, or whether we may have access to reproductive care, we need a way to instruct our elected officials at election time. If voters are to serve as the thermostat (Wlezien 1995) determining whether the government has gone too far or not far enough, they require meaningful party labels on the ballot. Pundits often lament the lack of an informed electorate, but parties are the instrument by which the electorate is informed.

So what exactly are the costs of attempting to reduce partisanship? Well, obviously, that would depend on the nature of the reform. If we're talking about turning a partisan legislature into a nonpartisan one (as Minnesota did in the 1910s and Nebraska did in the 1930s), the most immediate and likely result is lower voter turnout. When voters have a poorer understanding of the candidates and what they can be expected to do once in office, they are more likely to decline to even cast a vote. Assuming the presidential and congressional portions of the ballot remain partisan, similar numbers of voters will still vote in those elections, but rolloff to the state legislative races will likely increase substantially. Those voters who then decline to participate in the state legislative races will likely be among the more moderate voters, that is, the ones reformers would probably want to keep within the electorate.

Meanwhile, those voters that do stick around to vote in nonpartisan races will tend to be less informed than they were when the contest was partisan. Deprived of the party label, by far the most convenient shortcut to understanding what the candidates stand for, they will likely draw upon other available heuristics. Incumbency will be chief among these; the incumbency advantage can be expected to grow substantially under nonpartisanship. Voters may also make inferences based on the gender or perceived race of the candidates.

Antiparty reformers have, for more than a century, argued that removing party labels from a ballot will force voters to become more informed about the candidates and their stances. This claim flies in the face of all that we know about voters, who are, in the words of V. O. Key (1966), rationally ignorant. That is, they recognize that they are highly unlikely to cast a pivotal vote in any given election and thus have no incentive to pay the costs of becoming informed about politics. Relying on the "D" or "R" heuristic is an easy and generally reliable path for them. Deprive them of that, and they have no additional incentive to learn about candidates. It is always easier to decline to vote than to study candidates.

What if there were a less aggressive reform, such as an open primary (like in Wisconsin) or a top-two primary (like in Washington and California)? The chances are that little would actually change. We know that the people most likely to turn out in a primary election are already fairly partisan, so opening up participation to moderate independents won't do much to bring them into the mix. And, indeed, analysis of the top-two primary as adopted in California shows no impact on voter turnout, despite advocate's promises (Kousser 2015; Masket 2013c). Preliminary studies of the impact of the reform on polarization are notably mixed (Grose 2014; Sinclair 2015), but tend to indicate little change, if any.

One of the costs of such a reform, however, is an injury to registered partisans; it essentially deprives them of the power to select their party's nominees. This is not a trivial cost. As the US Supreme Court ruled in *California Democratic Party* v. *Jones*, when the state declares that anyone may participate in a primary (as it did under a "blanket" primary system in the late 1990s), including members of another party, it threatens to undermine the entire party system:

> [U]nder California's blanket primary system, the prospect of having a party's nominee determined by adherents of an opposing party is far from remote—indeed, it is a clear and present danger. . . . [A] single election in which the party nominee is selected by nonparty members could be enough to destroy the party.[2]

California figured out a way around this ruling for its top-two reform by including a provision in the initiative that redefined the summer election as a "voter-nomination primary election" rather than a party contest. In doing so, it deprived parties of their most important power, the selection of candidates for the general election ballot. Yet do not those who claim longstanding membership within a party maintain some legitimate claim over that party's survival? We know that "independent" voters are generally held in higher esteem by political observers than "partisan" ones. Yet this need not be our legal attitude toward them.

CONCLUSION

If party reform efforts tend to not only fail, but also impose costs on the political system in the form of lower turnout, more confusing and less meaningful elections, and declining accountability, what is the proper

---

2. *California Democratic Party* v. *Jones*, 530 U.S. 567 (2000).

way forward? Must we resign ourselves to accepting hyperpartisanship as the law of the land and learn to love the government shutdowns, debt limit breaches, filibusters, and recall elections that seem to go along with it?

The situation is not necessarily that dire. There are at least some modest reforms that have shown promise in mitigating partisanship that lack some of the nastier side-effects of the ones delineated above (Masket 2014). These could include ranked-choice voting (which has shown some ability to boost turnout and limit factionalism) or media reform (by which coverage of local politics might be improved, giving voters the tools to punish ideological extremism), among other things. But we'd need to temper our expectations. Even the most highly successful reforms would operate only at the margins. The ideologies that separate our parties run deep in American history, and there has probably never been a more perfect alignment between our liberal-conservative ideological divide and our Democratic-Republican party divide than there is right now (Noel 2013). To think that we could substantially undermine that by tinkering with election laws, redistricting reform, or by electing a "uniter" as president is wildly optimistic, at best.

The appropriate response may well be to adjust our institutions to meet our polarized parties, rather than depolarizing our parties to meet our institutions. That is, we know that polarization is not necessarily incompatible with governance. The 111th Congress (2009–2010) governed during a highly partisan period in recent American history and yet still managed to produce landmark legislation on the economy, health insurance, student loans, and other areas. It did so, of course, because it enjoyed a relatively rare period of unified party governance. Seen in this light, the problems of the last few years aren't due to polarization so much as to a divided governing structure. Conversely, as described above, California has experienced polarization and unified party government for many years, but nonetheless faced great budgetary problems because of an unusual two-thirds vote requirement for passing budgets. Seen in this light, the problem wasn't polarization so much as supermajority requirements.

All this is to say that polarized parties—which, let's recall, are the norm in American history rather than the exception—need not stand in the way of governance. Perhaps what is necessary is to allow majorities to govern by removing some of their impediments. Filibusters, debt ceiling votes, recall elections, supermajority requirements, and so forth, may certainly have their own justifications, but are they as valuable to us as the ability of a government to function? They are, after all, choices—sometimes aspects of state constitutions, sometimes laws, and sometimes just customs that have developed over the decades. They are hardly sacrosanct. And it is far easier to, say, eliminate the filibuster in a state legislature or even the US Senate than it is to compel our parties to be more moderate, and it has far fewer externalities.

But even as we consider all this, we shouldn't lose sight of the value that the party system offers our democracy. Despite the parties' unpopularity, they remain the greatest instruments for organizing elections, turning out voters, running government, and developing policy ideas and seeing them enacted that we've ever produced. At the very least, those who wish to weaken or abolish our parties should bear the burden of explaining why that is worth sacrificing.

Network Modeling in Nebraska

This section describes the exponential random graph model (ERGM), used to predict ties between actors in a network. ERGM functions like a logistic regression equation in networks research (Park and Newman 2004; Snijders et al. 2006; Wasserman and Pattison 1996). In essence, an ERGM investigates the differences between an observed network and a randomly generated network with an equal number of nodes (Cranmer, Desmarais, and Menninga 2012). It allows us to examine the impact of different variables on the likelihood of any two given nodes sharing a link, without concerns about the independence of cases.[1] In this particular case, we can assess the likelihood that any two nodes (candidates) in a network share a common donor, employing a variety of independent variables to predict this likelihood.

For this equation, I have used six independent variables:

1. Links: measuring the probability of observing a connection (also known as a "link" or an "edge") between any two candidates.
2. Party: comparing whether two candidates in a dyad are of the same party or not. This is based on the notion that two members of the same party would likely share a partisan donor.

1. The ERGM methodology assumes dependence among cases. As Cranmer and Desmarais (2011, 69) explain, "Instead of thinking about Y as a series of values drawn from a conditional univariate distribution (as is the case for standard regression models), we think of it as a single draw from a multivariate distribution where many other draws (many other realizations of the network) are possible. If Y is a single realization from a multivariate distribution, we no longer have to assume independence among the values of Y in any way."

3. Ideal point: measuring the absolute difference of the candidates' ideal points in a dyad, as calculated by Shor and McCarty. This is based on the idea that a donor would be likely to contribute to candidates of similar ideological persuasions, even if party itself is relatively meaningless.

4. Cohort: comparing whether two candidates in a dyad were elected the same year or not.

5. Lincoln/Omaha: comparing whether two candidates in a dyad are both from the state's major cities (Lincoln and Omaha) or both from rural areas, or if one is from an urban district and one is from a rural one.

6. Presidential year: comparing whether two candidates in a dyad were elected in a presidential year or not.

I add the network term "geometrically weight edgewise shared partner distribution" (GWESP) to this model, with an alpha value of zero. This helps control for the clustering and transitivity that tend to occur in networks of legislators. I expand the analysis by lowering the donation minimum to $500 in year 2000 dollars. This has the virtue of substantially increasing the number of cases—288 unique donors making 893 donations in 2000, rather than 45 unique donors making 106 donations— although the results from the analysis are substantively identical to those at the $2000 level. The analysis is limited to officeholders only. The models were estimated using the R packages Statnet and SNA. The results of the models appear in Table A1.

The coefficients are log-likelihoods, not lending themselves to easy interpretation, although their signs and levels of statistical significance are of interest. The main finding of note is that the party coefficient is statistically indistinguishable from zero in the years prior to term limits, and is actually in the wrong direction in 2004, suggesting that candidates of different parties were more likely to share a donor than those of the same party. In 2006 and 2008—after term limits have kicked in—the party coefficient is suddenly positive and statistically significant. (The coefficient is positive but not statistically significant in 2010.) For the sake of interpretation, the predicted probability of candidates sharing a donor

Table A1 ERGM Predicting Likelihood of Officeholders Sharing an Elite Donor, by Year

Variable	2000	2002	2004	2006	2008	2010
Links	−18.554***	0.477*	1.889	−17.363***	−18.640***	2.110***
	(0.134)	(0.223)	(1.069)	(0.129)	(0.192)	(0.148)
Party	0.110	0.608	-0.650	0.571**	0.647*	0.223
(node match)	(0.159)	(0.343)	(0.865)	(0.199)	(0.264)	(0.222)
Ideal point	−0.217	−0.354	−0.082	−0.022	0.368	−0.555**
(absolute difference)	(0.208)	(0.456)	(0.741)	(0.245)	(0.307)	(0.211)
Cohort	0.441	−0.037	0.764**	2.369***	0.571*	0.691*
(node match)	(0.272)	(0.407)	(0.811)	(0.365)	(0.277)	(0.242)
Lincoln/Omaha	0.486***	1.179***	−0.491*	0.215	−0.257	0.577***
(node factor)	(0.142)	(0.274)	(0.428)	(0.137)	(0.161)	(0.148)
Presidential year	0.146	1.304***	2.141***	−1.038***	1.132***	−0.560***
(node factor)	(0.126)	(0.324)	(0.518)	(0.156)	(0.247)	(0.159)
GWESP	19.476***	0.001	−1.117*	18.413***	18.401***	−0.697***
	(0.134)	(0.223)	(0.000)	(0.129)	(0.192)	(0.148)
Degrees of freedom	1,035	435	741	820	561	820
BIC	1173.5	352.9	1906.1	865.8	711.8	799.6

NOTES: Cell entries are exponential-family random graph model coefficients predicting the likelihood that any two given officeholders in the Nebraska legislature share an elite donor (contributing at least $500 in year 2000 dollars). Standard errors appear in parentheses beneath coefficients. Asterisks indicate statistical significance (* $p \leq .05$; ** $p \leq .01$; *** $p \leq .001$).

Table A2 TERGM PREDICTING LIKELIHOOD OF OFFICEHOLDERS
SHARING AN ELITE DONOR, 2000–2010

Variable	Coefficient
Links	−3.002*
	[−11.398 −1.840]
Party	−0.230
(edge cov.—match)	[−0.626 0.849]
Ideal point	−0.186
(absolute difference)	[−0.499 0.069]
Cohort	0.513*
(edge cov.—match)	[0.046 1.177]
Lincoln/Omaha	-0.122
(edge cov.—match)	[-0.322 0.044]
Presidential year	0.223
(edge cov.—match)	[−0.221 0.656]
Term limits	−0.409
(edge cov.—match)	[−0.929 0.163]
Party × term limits	0.644*
(edge cov.—match)	[0.184 1.128]
GWESP	2.601*
(set at 0.5)	[1.902 7.889]

NOTES: Cell entries are temporal exponential-family random graph model (TERGM) coefficients predicting the likelihood that any two given officeholders in the Nebraska legislature share an elite donor (contributing at least $500 in year 2000 dollars). 95 percent confidence intervals appear in brackets beneath coefficients. Asterisks indicate statistical significance (* $p \leq .05$).

if they are of the same party in 2000 is 49 percent, but 46 percent if they are of different parties. In 2008, conversely, that probability is 38 percent for those not sharing the same party and 53 percent for copartisans. These results suggest that party has become more important to structuring elite donations since the advent of term limits.[2]

2. These probabilities were calculated by holding the links, cohort, Lincoln/Omaha, and presidential year variables constant at 1 (i.e., the two members of a pair were of the same electoral cohort, were both either from or not from Lincoln/Omaha, and were both elected during a presidential year). The ideal point distance variable was held at 0.5. The geometrically weight edgewise shared partner distribution (GWESP) term is held at 0.9.

Ideology is in the expected direction, with ideologically similar candidates more likely to share a donor, but statistically significant in only one year—2010. We can understand this since only once the parties have polarized does it become possible for donors to distinguish between candidates in terms of ideology. The cohort variable is statistically significant from 2004 on, suggesting that the high turnover rates during this period produced increased attention by donors to new candidates. The region and presidential year coefficients vary a great deal from year to year with little apparent meaning.

Conducting the above analysis separately for each year may ignore some important time dependencies inherent in the network model. For example, the interaction of donors and candidates in one year may affect their interactions in future years. To account for these temporal dependencies, I have conducted a TERGM (temporal ERGM) analysis on the same data, combining all six observations from 2000 to 2010 into one network list. I add two new variables to the analysis here that were not in the previous one: a term limits variable (equaling zero from 2000 to 2004 and one from 2006 to 2010) and an interaction term for term limits and party. A positive coefficient on the interaction term would be consistent with the finding that party became a better predictor of sharing donors in the term limits era. The results for this TERGM can be found in Table A2. The results are consistent with expectations. The interaction term is positive and statistically significant at the $p \leq .05$ level.[3]

---

3. Analysis conducted using the XERGM package for R (version 1.0.4). The model converged with little difficulty and goodness-of-fit diagnostics are within acceptable parameters. Diagnostics and data are available from the author. XERGM does not report standard errors, so I have instead reported the 95 percent confidence intervals in the tables.

REFERENCES

Adler, E. Scott. 2002. *Why Congressional Reforms Fail: Reelection and the House Committee System*. American Politics and Political Economy. Chicago: University of Chicago Press.

Adrian, Charles R. 1952a. "General Characteristics of Nonpartisan Elections." *American Political Science Review* 46: 766–76.

———. 1952b. "The Origin of Minnesota's Nonpartisan Legislature." *Minnesota History* 33: 155–63.

Ahler, Douglas J., Jack Citrin, and Gabriel S. Lenz. 2015. "Why Voters May Have Failed to Reward Proximate Candidates in the 2012 Top Two Primary." *California Journal of Politics and Policy* 7. http://escholarship.org/uc/item/9714j8pc.

Ainsworth, Bill. 2003. "Four Top Democrats to Lay Low Should Davis Recall Qualify." *San Diego Union-Tribune*, June 18. A–3.

Aldrich, John H. 1983. "A Downsian Spatial Model with Party Activism." *American Political Science Review* 77: 974–90.

———. 1995. *Why Parties?* Chicago: University of Chicago Press.

Aldrich, John H., and James S. Coleman Battista. 2002. "Conditional Party Government in the States." *American Journal of Political Science* 46: 164–72.

Alter, Jonathan. 2009. "The Jackass-Reduction Plan." *Newsweek*, September 18: 29.

Ames, Michele. 2002. "'Big Money' Brouhaha No Laughing Matter – Both Sides Grit Teeth over Amendment on Campaign Finance." *Rocky Mountain News* (CO). 18A.

Ansolabehere, Stephen, Shigeo Hirano, James M. Snyder Jr., and Michiko Ueda. 2006. "Party and Incumbency Cues in Voting: Are They Substitutes?" *Quarterly Journal of Political Science* 1: 119–37.

Ansolabehere, Stephen, and Shanto Iyengar. 1995. *Going Negative: How Attack Ads Shrink and Polarize the Electorate*. New York: Free Press.

Ansolabehere, Stephen, Shanto Iyengar, Adam Simon, and Nicholas Valentino. 1994. "Does Attack Advertising Demobilize the Electorate?" *American Political Science Review* 88: 829–38.

Ansolabehere, Stephen, James M. Snyder Jr., and Charles Stewart III. 2001. "Candidate Positioning in U.S. House Elections." *American Journal of Political Science* 45: 136–59.

Bafumi, Joseph, and Michael C. Herron. 2010. "Leapfrog Representation and Extremism: A Study of American Voters and Their Members in Congress." *American Political Science Review* 104: 519–42.

Bailey, Delia, and Betsy Sinclair. 2009. "Partisan Polarization Via Term Limits: Political Networks in the CA Assembly." Paper presented at the the the annual meeting of the Midwest Political Science Association, Chicago, IL, April.

Bartels, Larry M., and John Zaller. 2001. "Presidential Vote Models: A Recount." *PS: Political Science and Politics* 34: 9–20.

Bawn, Kathleen, Marty Cohen, David Karol, Seth Masket, Hans Noel, and John Zaller. 2012. "A Theory of Political Parties: Groups, Policy Demands and Nominations in American Politics." *Perspectives on Politics* 10: 571–97.

Bean, Walton, and James J. Rawls. 1983. *California: An Interpretive History.* New York: McGraw-Hill Book Company.

Beck, Paul Allen. 1997. *Party Politics in America.* 8th ed. New York: Longman.

Beer, Caroline. 2001. "Assessing the Consequences of Electoral Democracy: Subnational Legislative Change in Mexico." *Comparative Politics* 33: 421–40.

Bender, Michael C. 2002. "Campaign-Finance Reform 'Answer to What Ails Politics'." *Daily Sentinel* (Grand Junction, CO), September 22.

Berelson, Bernard R., Paul F. Lazarsfeld, and William N. McPhee. 1954. *Voting: A Study of Opinion Formation in a Presidential Campaign.* Chicago: University of Chicago Press.

Bernstein, Jonathan. 1999. "The Expanded Party in American Politics." PhD diss., University of California, Berkeley.

Boatright, Robert. 2013. *Getting Primaried: The Changing Politics of Congressional Primary Challenges.* Ann Arbor: University of Michigan Press.

Bonica, Adam. 2013. Database on Ideology, Money in Politics, and Elections: Public Version 1.0. Stanford, CA: Stanford University.

Booth, Michael. 2002. "Campaign Finance: Coloradans Support Limits on Political Donations." *Denver Post*, November 6, E-03.

Brandt, Edward R. 1977. "Legislative Voting Behavior in Minnesota." In *Perspectives on Minnesota Government and Politics*, ed. Millard L. Gieske and Edward R. Brandt. Dubuque, IA: Kendall/Hunt, 202–22.

Buchanan, Wyatt, and Carolyn Jones. 2010. "Voters Approve Prop. 14, Open Primary Measure." *San Francisco Chronicle*, June 9. http://www.sfgate.com/politics/article/Voters-approve-Prop-14-open-primary-measure-3185971.php.

Bullock, Charles S., III, and Richard E. Dunn. 1996. "Election Roll-Off: A Test of Three Explanations." *Urban Affairs Review* 32: 71–86.

Burke, Edmund. [1790] 1973. *Reflections on the Revolution in France.* New York: Anchor.

Burnett, Sara. 2006. "State Ed Board Member Polis Announces He's Gay." *Rocky Mountain News*, July 6, 10A.

Cahn, Emily. 2013. "Old-School Politics Reign in California's New Primary." *Roll Call*, June 10. http://www.rollcall.com/news/old_school_politics_reign_in_californias_new_primary-225495-1.html

Cain, Bruce E., and Thad Kousser. 2004. *Adapting to Term Limits: Recent Experiences and New Directions.* San Francisco: Public Policy Institute of California.

California Secretary of State. 2010. "Official Voter Information Guide." Sacramento.

Campbell, Angus, Philip E. Converse, Warren E. Miller, and Donald E. Stokes. 1960. *The American Voter.* New York: John Wiley and Sons.

Cohen, Marty, David Karol, Hans Noel, and John Zaller. 2008. *The Party Decides: Presidential Nominations before and after Reform.* Chicago Studies in American Politics. Chicago: University of Chicago Press.

Colorado Springs Gazette. 2008. "Take Our 'Shall I Vote?' Quiz." November 3.

Cox, Gary W. 1987. *The Efficient Secret: The Cabinet and the Development of Political Parties in Victorian England.* Cambridge: Cambridge University Press.

Cox, Gary W., and Mathew D. McCubbins. 1993. *Legislative Leviathan: Party Government in the House.* Berkeley: University of California Press.

———. 2005. *Setting the Agenda: Responsible Party Government in the U.S. House of Representatives.* Cambridge; New York: Cambridge University Press.

Cranmer, Skyler J., and Bruce A. Desmarais. 2011. "Inferential Network Analysis with Exponential Random Graph Models." *Political Analysis* 19: 66–86.

Cranmer, Skyler J., Bruce A. Desmarais, and Elizabeth J. Menninga. 2012. "Complex Dependencies in the Alliance Network." *Conflict Management and Peace Science* 29: 279–313.

Cronin, Thomas E. 1989. *Direct Democracy: The Politics of Initiative, Referendum, and Recall.* Cambridge, MA: Harvard University Press.

Crummy, Karen E. 2012. "Spending by Super Pacs in Colorado Is the Dominion of Democrats." *Denver Post*, March 10.

Delli Carpini, Michael X., and Scott Keeter. 1993. "Measuring Political Knowledge: Putting First Things First." *American Journal of Political Science* 37: 1179–206.

Diermeier, Daniel. 1995. "Commitment, Deference, and Legislative Institutions." *American Political Science Review* 89: 344–55.

DiSalvo, Daniel. 2012. *Engines of Change: Party Factions in American Politics, 1868–2010.* Oxford: Oxford University Press.

Doherty, Joseph William. 2006. "The Candidate-Consultant Network in California Legislative Campaigns: A Social Network Analysis of Informal Party Organization." PhD diss., University of California.

Dominguez, Casey Byrne Knudsen. 2005. "Before the Primary: Party Participation in Congressional Nominating Processes." PhD diss., University of California, Berkeley.

Downs, Anthony. 1957. *An Economic Theory of Democracy.* New York: Harper and Row.

Elazar, Daniel J., Virginia Gray, and Wyman Spano. 1999. *Minnesota Politics and Government.* Lincoln: University of Nebraska Press.

Elias, Thomas D. 2009. "Open Primary Should Be Top 2010 Voter Priority." *Ventura County Star*, December 18. http://www.vcstar.com/opinion/open-primary-should-be-top-2010-voter-priority-ep-370231832-350301141.html

Epstein, Leon D. 1967. *Political Parties in Western Democracies.* New York: Praeger.

Finkel, Steven E. 1993. "Reexamining the 'Minimal Effects' Model in Recent Presidential Campaigns." *Journal of Politics* 55: 1–21.

Fish, Sandra. 2002. "Amendment 27 Would Change Funding Landscape—Parties, Candidates Would Have Millions Less If Limits Were in Effect This Year." *Daily Camera* (Boulder, CO), October 31. A2.

Fjelstad, Ralph S. 1955. "How About Party Labels?" *National Municipal Review* 44: 359–64.

Franz, Michael. 2013. "Bought and Sold: The High Price of the Permanent Campaign." *American Interest* (July/August).

Galvin, Daniel J. 2012. "The Transformation of Political Institutions: Investments in Institutional Resources and Gradual Change in the National Party Committees." *Studies in American Political Development* 26: 50–70.

Gelman, Andrew, and Gary King. 1993. "Why Are American Presidential Election Campaign Polls So Variable When Votes Are So Predictable?" *British Journal of Political Science* 23: 409–51.

Gerber, Alan S., and Donald P. Green. 2000. "The Effects of Canvassing, Telephone Calls, and Direct Mail on Voter Turnout: A Field Experiment." *American Political Science Review* 94: 653–63.

———. 2005. "Correction to Gerber and Green (2000), Replication of Disputed Findings, and Reply to Imai." *American Political Science Review* 99: 301–13.

Gerber, Elisabeth R., and Rebecca B. Morton. 1998. "Primary Election Systems and Representation." *Journal of Law, Economics and Organization* 14: 304–24.

Graf, Joseph, and Grant Reeher. 2006. *Small Donors and Online Giving: A Study of Donors to the 2004 Presidential Campaigns*. Washington, DC: Campaign Finance Institute, and Institute for Politics, Democracy and the Internet.

Grose, Christian. 2014. "The Adoption of Electoral Reforms and Ideological Change in the California State Legislature." USC Schwarzenegger Institute Report.

Groseclose, Tim, Steven D. Levitt, and James M. Snyder. 1999. "Comparing Interest Group Scores across Time and Chambers: Adjusted A.D.A. Scores for the U.S. Congress." *American Political Science Review* 98: 33–50.

Hacker, Jacob S. 2002. *The Divided Welfare State*. Cambridge: Cambridge University Press.

Hall, Andrew B. 2014. "How the Public Funding of Elections Increases Candidate Polarization." Harvard University, Typescript.

Harmel, Robert, and Kenneth Janda. 1982. *Parties and Their Environments: Limits to Reform?* New York: Longman.

Harvey, Anna, and Bumba Mukherjee. 2006. "Electoral Institutions and the Evolution of Partisan Conventions, 1880–1940." *American Politics Research* 34: 368–98.

Hassell, Hans J. G. 2013. "The Non-Existent Primary-Ideology Link, or Do Open Primaries Actually Limit Party Influence in Primary Elections?" Paper presented at the 13th annual State Politics and Policy Conference, Iowa City, Iowa, May 24.

Hathaway, William L., and Millard L. Gieske. 1985. "Minnesota Political Parties and Politics." In *Perspectives on Minnesota Government and Politics*, ed. Millard L. Gieske. 2nd ed. Minneapolis, MN: Burgess, 53–81.

Hershey, Marjorie Randon. 2013. "Third Parties: How American Law and Institutions Cripple Third Parties." In *Law and Election Politics*, ed. Matthew J. Streb. New York: Routledge, 208–29.

Hillygus, D. Sunshine, and Simon Jackman. 2003. "Voter Decision Making in Elections 2000: Campaign Effects, Partisan Activation, and the Clinton Legacy." *American Journal of Political Science* 47: 583–96.

Hofstadter, Richard. 1955. *The Age of Reform: From Bryan to FDR*. Vol. 95. New York: Random House.

———. 1972. *The Idea of a Party System*. Berkeley: University of California Press.

Huber, Evelyne, and John D. Stephens. 2001. *Development and Crisis of the Welfare State*. Chicago: University of Chicago Press.

Imai, Kosuke. 2005. "Do Get-out-the-Vote Calls Reduce Turnout? The Importance of Statistical Methods for Field Experiments." *American Political Science Review* 99: 283–300.

Jacobson, Gary C., and Samuel Kernell. 1981. *Strategy and Choice in Congressional Elections*. New Haven, CT: Yale University Press.

Jenkins, Jeffery A. 2000. "Examining the Robustness of Ideological Voting: Evidence from the Confederate House of Representatives." *American Journal of Political Science* 44: 811–22.

Jewell, Malcolm Edwin. 1982. *Representation in State Legislatures*. Lexington: University Press of Kentucky.

Kanthak, Kristin, and Rebecca Morton. 2001. "The Effects of Electoral Rules on Congressional Primaries." In *Congressional Primaries and the Politics of Representation*, ed. Peter F. Galderisis, Marni Ezra, and Michael Lyons. Lanham, MD: Rowman and Littlefield, 113–31.

Keith, Bruce E., David B. Magelby, Candice J. Nelson, Elizabeth Orr, Mark C. Westlye, and Raymond E. Wofinger. 1992. *The Myth of the Independent Voter*. Berkeley: University of California Press.

Kent, Frank R. 1924. *The Great Game of Politics: An Effort to Present the Elementary Human Facts About Politics, Politicians, and Political Machines, Candidates and Their Ways*. Garden City, NY: Doubleday, Page.

Key, V. O., Jr. 1952. *Politics, Parties, and Pressure Groups*. Vol. 3. New York: Thomas Y. Crowell.

———. 1949. *Southern Politics*. New York: Vintage.

Key, V. O., and Milton C. Cummings. 1966. *The Responsible Electorate: Rationality in Presidential Voting, 1936–1960*. Cambridge, MA: Belknap Press of Harvard University Press.

Klinghard, Daniel. 2010. *The Nationalization of American Political Parties, 1880–1896*. New York: Cambridge University Press.

Koger, Gregory, Seth E. Masket, and Hans Noel. 2009. "Partisan Webs: Information Exchange and Party Networks." *British Journal of Political Science* 39: 633–53.

———. 2010. "Cooperative Party Factions in American Politics." *American Politics Research* 38: 33–53.

Kousser, Thad. 2015. "The Top-Two, Take Two: Did Changing the Rules Change the Game in Statewide Contests?" *California Journal of Politics and Policy* 7. http://escholarship.org/uc/item/63w1x0f8.

Kousser, Thad, Scott Lucas, Seth Masket, and Eric McGhee. 2015. "Kingmakers or Cheerleaders? Party Power and the Causal Effects of Endorsements." *Political Research Quarterly* 68: 443–56.

Kousser, Thad, Justin H. Phillips, and Boris Shor. 2016. "Reform and Representation: Assessing California's Top-Two Primary and Redistricting Commission." *Political Science Research and Methods* (forthcoming).

Kurtz, Karl T., Bruce E. Cain, and Richard G. Niemi. 2007. *Institutional Change in American Politics: The Case of Term Limits*. Ann Arbor: University of Michigan Press.

Kurtzman, Laura, and Howard Mintz. 2003. "State Party Set to Back Bustamante." *San Jose Mercury News*, August 28, 1A.

La Raja, Raymond, and Brian F. Schaffner. 2015. *Campaign Finance and Political Polarization: When Purists Prevail*. Ann Arbor: University of Michigan Press.

LaVelle, Philip J. 2003. "Bustamante Support Grows State's Democrats in Congress, Union of Teachers Join Fold." *San Diego Union-Tribune*, August 22, A1.

Lawrence, Eric, Todd Donovan, and Shaun Bowler. 2013. "The Adoption of Direct Primaries in the United States." *Party Politics* 19: 3–18.

Layman, Geoffrey C., and Thomas M. Carsey. 2002. "Party Polarization and 'Conflict Extension' in the American Electorate." *American Journal of Political Science* 46: 786–802.

Leavitt, Donald. 1977. "Changing Rules, Norms and Procedures in the Minnesota Legislature." In *Perspectives on Minnesota Government and Politics*, ed. Millard L. Gieske and Edward R. Brandt. Dubuque, IA: Kendall/Hunt, 185–201.

Legislative Council of the Colorado General Assembly. 2002. "2002 Ballot Information Booklet." Denver.

Levitt, Steven D. 1994. "Using Repeat Challengers to Estimate the Effect of Campaign Spending on Election Outcomes in the U.S. House." *Journal of Political Economy* 102: 777–98.

Lewis-Beck, Michael S., and Tom W. Rice. 1992. *Forecasting Elections*. Washington, DC: CQ Press.

Lovejoy, Allen Fraser. 1941. *La Follette and the Establishment of the Direct Primary in Wisconsin, 1890–1904*. New Haven, CT: Yale University Press.

Manning, Eric. 2004. "The Effects of a Nonpartisan and Partisan Legislature on Legislative Output: The Case of Minnesota." Paper presented at the the annual conference of the Southern Political Science Association, New Orleans, January 8.

———. 2005. "How Important Are Parties in Legislatures? Legislative Behavior in Partisan and Non-Partisan Settings." Paper presented at the the annual State Politics and Policy Conference, East Lansing, MI, May 13–14.

Masket, Seth E. 2009a. "Did Obama's Ground Game Matter? The Influence of Local Field Offices During the 2008 Presidential Election." *Public Opinion Quarterly* 73: 1023–39.

———. 2009b. *No Middle Ground: How Informal Party Organizations Control Nominations and Polarize Legislatures*. Ann Arbor: University of Michigan Press.

———. 2011. "The Circus That Wasn't: The Republican Party's Quest for Order in the 2003 California Gubernatorial Recall." *State Politics and Policy Quarterly* 11: 124–48.

———. 2013a. "The Networked Party: How Social Network Analysis Is Revolutionizing the Study of Political Parties." In *New Directions in American Politics*, ed. Raymond J. La Raja. New York: Routledge, 107–24.

———. 2013b. "Picking a State? The Stakes Are Getting Higher." *Al Jazeera America*, November 27.

———. 2013c. "Polarization Interrupted? California's Experiment with the Top-Two Primary." In *Governing California: Politics, Government, and Public Policy in the Golden State*, ed. Ethan Rarick, 3rd ed. Berkeley: Institute for Government Studies, 175–92.

———. 2014. *Mitigating Extreme Partisanship in an Era of Networked Parties: An Examination of Various Reform Strategies*. Washington, DC: Brookings Institution.

Masket, Seth, and Michael Miller. 2015. "Does Public Election Funding Create More Extreme Legislators? Evidence from Arizona and Maine." *State Politics and Policy Quarterly* 15: 24–40.

Masket, Seth E., and Hans Noel. 2012. "Serving Two Masters: Using Referenda to Assess Partisan Versus Dyadic Legislative Representation." *Political Research Quarterly* 65: 104–23.

Masket, Seth E., and Boris Shor. 2015. "Polarization without Parties: Term Limits and Legislative Partisanship in Nebraska's Unicameral Legislature." *State Politics and Policy Quarterly* 15: 67–90.

Mathews, Joe. 2006. *The People's Machine: Schwarzenegger and the Rise of Blockbuster Democracy*. New York: Public Affairs.

Mayhew, David R. 1974. *Congress: The Electoral Connection*. New Haven, CT: Yale University Press.

McGhee, Eric. 2010. *Open Primaries*. San Francisco: Public Policy Institute of California.

McGhee, Eric, Seth Masket, Boris Shor, Steven Rogers, and Nolan McCarty. 2014. "A Primary Cause of Partisanship? Nomination Systems and Legislator Ideology." *American Journal of Political Science* 58: 337–51.

Miller, Michael. 2013. *Subsidizing Democracy: How Public Funding Changes Elections, and How It Can Work in the Future*. Ithaca, NY: Cornell University Press.

Mitau, G. Theodore. 1960. *Politics in Minnesota*. Minneapolis: University of Minnesota Press.

———. 1970. *Politics in Minnesota*. 2nd rev. ed. Minneapolis: University of Minnesota Press.

Mowry, George Edwin. 1951. *The California Progressives*. Chicago: Quadrangle.

National Conference of State Legislatures (NCSL). 2015. "State Partisan Composition." http://www.ncsl.org/research/about-state-legislatures/partisan-composition.aspx.

Niemi, Richard G., and Lynda W. Powell. 2004. "Time, Term Limits, and Turnover: Trends in Membership Stability in U.S. State Legislatures." *Legislative Studies Quarterly* 29: 357–81.

Noel, Hans. 2011. "Toward a Theory of Parties *as* Networks." Paper presented at the the annual conference of the American Political Science Association, Seattle, Washington, September 3.

———. 2013. *Political Ideologies and Political Parties in America*. Cambridge: Cambridge University Press.

Orlov, Rick. 2003. "Recall Election: Garamendi Drops Out." *Inland Valley Daily Bulletin*, August 9.

Ostrogorski, Mosei, and Frederick Clarke. 1902. *Democracy and the Organization of Political Parties*. New York: Macmillan.

Park, Juyong, and M. E. J. Newman. 2004. "The Statistical Mechanics of Networks." *Physical Review E* 70: 066117.

Persily, Nathaniel A. 1997. "The Peculiar Geography of Direct Democracy: Why the Initiative, Referendum and Recall Developed in the American West." *Michigan Law and Policy Review* 11: 21–32.

Philipp, Emanuel L. 1910. *Political Reform in Wisconsin: A Historical Review of the Subjects of Primary Election, Taxation and Railway Regulation.* Madison: State Historical Society of Wisconsin.

Pierson, Paul. 2005. "The Study of Policy Development." *Journal of Policy History* 17: 34–51.

Polsby, Nelson W., Aaron B. Wildavsky, and David A. Hopkins. 2008. *Presidential Elections: Strategies and Structures of American Politics.* 12th ed. Lanham, MD: Rowman and Littlefield.

Poole, Keith, Jeffrey Lewis, James Lo, and Royce Carroll. 2014. "Package 'Wnominate.'" *Comprehensive R Archive Network.* https://cran.r-project.org/web/packages/wnominate/index.html.

Poole, Keith T. 2003. "Changing Minds? Not in Congress!" In *Working Paper #1997-22*: Carnegie-Mellon University.

Progressive Party. 1912. "1912 Progressive Party Platform." *The American Presidency Project.* http://www.presidency.ucsb.edu/ws/?pid=29617.

Ranney, Austin. 1975. *Curing the Mischiefs of Faction: Party Reform in America.* Jefferson Memorial Lectures. Berkeley: University of California Press.

Reynolds, John Francis. 2006. *The Demise of the American Convention System, 1880–1911.* Cambridge: Cambridge University Press.

Rodgers, Jack, Robert Sittig, and Susan Welch. 1984. "The Legislature." In *Nebraska Government and Politics*, ed. Robert D. Miewald. Lincoln: University of Nebraska Press. 57–86.

Rogers, Steven. 2013. "Accountability in a Federal System." PhD diss., Princeton University.

Roosevelt, Theodore. 1906. "Machine Politics in New York City." In *American Ideals and Other Essays, Social and Political.* New York: Scribner. 112–46.

Rosenblum, Nancy L. 2008. *On the Side of the Angels: An Appreciation of Parties and Partisanship.* Princeton, NJ: Princeton University Press.

Rosenstone, Steven J. 1983. *Forecasting Presidential Elections.* New Haven, CT: Yale University Press.

Rutland, Robert Allen. 1995. *The Democrats from Jefferson to Clinton.* Columbia: University of Missouri Press.

Sartori, Giovanni. 1976. *Parties and Party Systems: A Framework for Analysis.* Cambridge: Cambridge University Press.

Schaffner, Brian F., and Matthew Streb. 2002. "The Partisan Heuristic in Low-Information Elections." *Public Opinion Quarterly* 54: 7–30.

Schaffner, Brian F., Matthew Streb, and Gerald C. Wright. 2001. "Teams without Uniforms: The Nonpartisan Ballot in State and Local Elections." *Political Research Quarterly* 54: 7–30.

Schattschneider, E. E. 1935. *Politics, Pressures and the Tariff: A Study of Free Private Enterprise in Pressure Politics, as Shown in the 1929–1930 Revision of the Tariff.* New York: Prentice-Hall.

———. 1942. *Party Government.* Westport, CT: Greenwood Press.

Schlesinger, Joseph A. 1984. "On the Theory of Party Organization." *Journal of Politics* 46: 369–400.

———. 1991. *Political Parties and the Winning of Office.* Ann Arbor: University of Michigan Press.

Schrager, Adam, and Rob Witwer. 2010. *The Blueprint: How Democrats Won the West (and Why Republicans Should Care).* Golden, CO: Fulcrum.

Schulte, Grant. 2014. "Nebraska Lawmakers Vote to Override Budget Vetoes." *Associated Press State Wire*, April 1.

Schwartz, Thomas. 1989. "Why Parties?". Typescript. Department of Political Science, University of California, Los Angeles.

Seitz, Steven Thomas, and L. Earl Shaw Jr. 1985. "Partisanship in a Nonpartisan Legislature: Minnesota." In *Perspectives on Minnesota Government and Politics*, ed. Millard L. Gieske. 2nd ed. Minneapolis: Burgess. 147–55.

Serra, Gilles. 2011. "Why Primaries? The Party's Tradeoff between Policy and Valence." *Journal of Theoretical Politics* 23: 21–51.

———. 2015. "No Polarization in Spite of Primaries: A Median Voter Theorem with Competitive Nominations." In *The Political Economy of Governance: Institutions, Political Performance and Elections*, ed. Norman Schofield and Gonzalo Caballero. Basel: Springer, 211–29

Shaw, Daron R. 1999. "The Effect of T.V. Ads and Candidate Appearances on Statewide Presidential Votes, 1988–96." *American Political Science Review* 93: 345–61.

Sheppard, Harrison. 2003. "Labor Federation Reverses Course on Recall—Powerful Group Throws Support to Bustamante." *Inland Valley Daily Bulletin*, August 26.

Shor, Boris, Christopher Berry, and Nolan McCarty. 2010. "A Bridge to Somewhere: Mapping State and Congressional Ideology on a Cross-Institutional Common Space." *Legislative Studies Quarterly* 35: 417–48.

Shor, Boris, and Nolan McCarty. 2011. "The Ideological Mapping of American Legislatures." *American Political Science Review* 105: 530–51.

———. 2013. "Individual State Legislator Shor-McCarty Ideology Data." Version 1. *Harvard Dataverse Network.* http://hdl.handle.net/1902.1/21509.

Silver, Nate. 2008. "The Contact Gap: Proof of the Importance of the Ground Game?" *FiveThirtyEight.com.* http://www.fivethirtyeight.com/2008/11/contact-gap- proof-of- importance-of.html.

Sinclair, Betsy. 2015. "Introduction: The California Top Two Primary." *California Journal of Politics and Policy* 7: 1–6.

Sittig, Robert. 1986. *The Nebraska Unicameral after Fifty Years.* Lincoln: University of Nebraska.

Skinner, Richard M., Seth E. Masket, and David A. Dulio. 2012. "527s and the Political Party Network." *American Politics Research* 40: 60–84.

Skocpol, Theda, and Paul Pierson. 2002. "Historical Institutionalism in Contemporary Political Science." In *Political Science: State of the Discipline*, ed. Ira Katznelson and Helen V. Milner. New York: W. W. Norton, 693–721.

Smith, Jennifer K., and Julia R. Azari. 2015. "The Anti-Party Tradition in American Political Development." In *Working paper*.

Snijders, Tom A. B., Philippa E. Pattison, Garry L. Robins, and Mark S. Handcock. 2006. "New Specifications for Exponential Random Graph Models." *Sociological Methodology* 36: 99–153.

Squire, Peverill, and Eric R. A. N. Smith. 1988. "The Effect of Partisan Information on Voters in Nonpartisan Elections." *Journal of Politics* 50: 169–79.

Steers, Stuart. 2006. "Dem Quartet's 527 Aid Building Success for Party." *Rocky Mountain News*, September 5, 14A.

Steffens, Lincoln. 1904. *The Shame of the Cities*. New York: McClure, Phillips.

Straumanis, Andris. 1994. "Partisan Politics." *Session Weekly*. http://www.house.leg. state.mn.us/hinfo/swkly/1995-96/select/party.txt.

Thistlethwaite, Donald L., and Donald T. Campbell. 1960. "Regression Discontinuity Analysis: An Alternative to the Ex-Post Facto Experiment." *Journal of Educational Psychology* 51: 309–17.

Transparency International. 2013. "Global Corruption Barometer 2013: Report." http://www.transparency.org/gcb2013/report.

Trounstine, Jessica. 2008. *Political Monopolies in American Cities: The Rise and Fall of Bosses and Reformers*. Chicago: University of Chicago Press.

Unger, Nancy C. 2000. *Fighting Bob La Follette: The Righteous Reformer*. Chapel Hill: University of North Carolina Press.

Van Oot, Torey. 2011. "Republican Chairman Pushing for New Nominating Process." CapitolAlert, *Sacramento Bee*, February 15. http://blogs.sacbee.com/capitolalertlat-est/2011/02/crp-chair-ron-nehring.html.

Vocke , William C., Jr. 2010. "Open Primaries: William Vocke Interviews Abel Maldonado, Lieutenant Governor of California." Carnegie Council for Ethics in International Affairs, April 29. http://www.carnegiecouncil.org/es/studio/multime-dia/20100429/index.html.

Ware, Alan. 2002. *The American Direct Primary*. New York: Cambridge University Press.

Wasserman, Stanley, and Phillipa Pattison. 1996. "Logit Models and Logistic Regression for Social Networks: I. An Introduction to Markov Graphs and P^*." *Psychometrica* 61: 401–25.

Wattenberg, Martin P., Ian McAllister, and Anthony Salvanto. 2000. "How Voting Is Like Taking an S.A.T. Test: An Analysis of American Voter Rolloff." *American Politics Research* 28: 234–50.

Weinstein, Rachel. 2005. "You're Fired! The Voters' Version of *The Apprentice*: An Analysis of Local Recall Elections in California." *Southern California Interdisciplinary Law Journal* 15: 131–64.

Welch, Susan, and Timothy Bledsoe. 1986. "The Partisan Consequences of Nonpartisan Elections and the Changing Nature of Urban Politics." *American Journal of Political Science* 30: 128–39.

Welch, Susan, and Eric H. Carlson. 1973. "The Impact of Party Voting Behavior in a Nonpartisan Legislature." *American Political Science Review* 67: 854–67.

Wiebe, Robert H. 1967. *The Search for Order, 1877–1920*. Westport, CT: Greenwood.

Winona Daily News. 1970a. "Anderson Flays G.O.P. Party Stand." April 2, 13.

———. 1970b. "D.F.L. District Convention Action Favors Pre-Primary Endorsing." May 11, 3.

———. 1970c. "Nonpartisan Legislature Causes Its Share of Laughs in Minnesota." April 22.

———. 1971. "L.W.V. Slates Petition Campaign." March 10, 23.

Witwer, Rob. 2009. "Rocky Ride: The Republicans' Fall from Power in Colorado—and How the Democrats Hope to Replicate It." *National Review*, March 23.

Wlezien, Christopher. 1995. "The Public as Thermostat: Dynamics of Preferences for Spending." *American Journal of Political Science* 39: 981–1000.

Wright, Gerald C., Tracy Osborn, and Jon Winburn. 2004. "Patterns of Roll Call Voting in America's Legislatures." Paper presented at the the annual conference of the Midwest Political Science Association, Chicago.

Wright, Gerald C., and Brian F. Schaffner. 2002. "The Influence of Party: Evidence from the State Legislatures." *American Political Science Review* 96: 367–79.

Yglesias, Matthew. 2009. "Gerrymandering and Polarization." *Think Progress*, October 1. http://thinkprogress.org/yglesias/2009/10/01/194566/gerrymandering-and-polarization/.

Numbers in **bold** indicate pages with figures and tables